Golf GTI Mk I

MIKE BREWER'S THE WHEELER DEALER KNOW HOW!

VELOCE PUBLISHING
THE PUBLISHER OF FINE AUTOMOTIVE BOOKS

Also from Veloce Publishing

Speedpro Series
Ford V8, How to Power Tune Small Block Engines (Hammill)
Land Rover Discovery, Defender & Range Rover – How to Modify Coil
   Sprung Models for High Performance & Off-Road Action (Hosier)
Mini Engines, How to Power Tune On a Small Budget – Colour Edition
   (Hammill)
Volkswagen Beetle Suspension, Brakes & Chassis, How to Modify For
   High Performance (Hale)

Enthusiast's Restoration Manual Series
Jaguar E-type (Crespin)
Volkswagen Beetle, How to Restore (Tyler)

Expert Guides
Land Rover Series I-III – Your expert guide to common problems &
   how to fix them (Thurman)

Essential Buyer's Guide Series
Citroën ID & DS (Heilig)
Ford Capri (Paxton)
Jaguar E-type 3.8 & 4.2-litre (Crespin)
Jaguar E-type V12 5.3-litre (Crespin)
Land Rover Series I, II & IIA (Thurman)
Mazda MX-5 Miata (Mk1 1989-97 & Mk2 98-2001) (Crook)
Mercedes-Benz 280-560SL & SLC (W107 series Roadsters & Coupes
   1971 to 1989) (Bass)
MGA 1955-1962 (Sear, Crosier)
Mini (Paxton)
Peugeot 205 GTI (Blackburn)
Porsche 911 (930) Turbo series (Streather)
Triumph Spitfire & GT6 (Baugues)
VW Beetle (Cservenka & Copping)
VW Golf GTI (Cservenka & Copping)

Those Were The Days ... Series
American 'Independent' Automakers – AMC to Willys 1945 to 1960
   (Mort)

Rally Giants Series
Ford Escort MkI (Robson)
Mini Cooper/Mini Cooper S (Robson)
Peugeot 205 T16 (Robson)

General
Anatomy of the Works Minis (Moylan)
Automotive A-Z, Lane's Dictionary of Automotive Terms (Lane)
Bentley MkVI, Rolls-Royce Silver Wraith, Dawn & Cloud/Bentley R &
   S-Series (Nutland)
British Cars, The Complete Catalogue of, 1895-1975 (Culshaw &
   Horrobin)
Citroën DS (Bobbitt)
Dodge Charger – Enduring Thunder (Ackerson)
Dodge Dynamite! (Grist)
Ford Cleveland 335-Series V8 engine 1970 to 1982 – The Essential
   Source Book (Hammill)
Karmann-Ghia Coupé & Convertible (Bobbitt)
Mazda MX-5/Miata 1.6 Enthusiast's Workshop Manual (Grainger &
   Shoemark)
Mazda MX-5/Miata 1.8 Enthusiast's Workshop Manual (Grainger &
   Shoemark)
Mazda MX-5 Miata: The Book of the World's Favourite Sportscar
   (Long)
Mazda MX-5 Miata Roadster (Long)
Maximum Mini (Booij)
MGA (Price Williams)
Mini Cooper – The Real Thing! (Tipler)
Porsche 911, The Book of the (Long)
SM – Citroën's Maserati-engined Supercar (Long & Claverol)
VW Beetle Cabriolet – The full story of the convertible Beetle (Bobbitt)
VW Beetle – The Car of the 20th Century (Copping)
VW Golf: Five Generations of Fun (Copping & Cservenka)
VW – The Air-cooled Era (Copping)

www.veloce.co.uk

First published in April 2013 by Veloce Publishing Limited, Veloce House, Parkway Farm Business Park, Middle Farm Way, Poundbury, Dorchester, Dorset, DT1 3AR, England. Fax 01305 250479/e-mail info@veloce.co.uk/web www.veloce.co.uk or www.velocebooks.com.

ISBN: 978-1-845844-89-9 UPC: 6-36847-04489-3

The images used in this book are reproduced with the kind permission of:
Jack Barnes (cover picture); Auto Express magazine; Bentley Motors; Chrysler Group LLC; Citroën UK; Daimler AG; Daniel Allum (Willys Jeep and Ford Mustang); Ford Motor Company; Honda UK; James Cheadle (DeLorean; Dodge Charger; Jaguar E-Type; Land Rover; Lotus Elan; Morgan; Ferrari 308); James Sheppard (Ford Capri); John Figg (Karmann Ghia); Jonathan Braim (Porsche 911); Jonathan Yarwood, Club Peugeot UK (Peugeot 205 GTi); Land Rover UK; Mazda UK; Mike Rowntree (Triumph Spitfire); Neil at Automac (BMW 3 Series); Paul Rider (Mercedes G-Wagen); Pete Dadds (Chevrolet Bel Air; Chevrolet pickup); Peugeot UK; Richard Ladds, MG Owners Club (MGA); Steve Fermor, Jaguar Drivers Club (Daimler Double Six); Vauxhall Motors UK; Volkswagen UK.

CONTENTS

8th June 1959-8th October 2010
"You inspired me"

and

Patricia Turvey (Mum)
29th May 1940-19th August 2012
"You made me smile every day"

INTRODUCTION

Welcome to *The Wheeler Dealer Know How*, the book that will tell you everything you need to know about buying, owning, and selling a modern classic.

Right from my earliest years growing up in Brixton I've absolutely loved cars. My dad was a famous car customiser back in his heyday, so I reckon that's where I must have got it from. He had loads of interesting motors over the years (and probably a few rubbish ones as well) and I can remember feeling so excited when he was taking me to school in his latest favourite. With older brothers and sisters in the family, I had plenty of people to learn from when it came to cars and driving, so I was never short of inspiration, and I'll never forget the great times I had cruising around London with my brothers. And where did all this lead? To being a wheeler dealer, of course!

You probably know me best from television, but that's not how I started, not by a long way. For that, you have to go back to the heady days of the 1980s and a smoky snooker hall in southwest London (I know, snooker is a long way from car dealing but bear with me on this), for that's when I got the break that would launch me on the road to becoming a wheeler dealer!

I was managing a snooker hall when in walked the guy that was to change my life forever. Peter Stapleton (known to everyone as 'Budgie' as he was a dead ringer for Adam Faith), and his partner John Henson (known as the 'Major'), owned the used car heaven that was St Georges Garages in Tooting, a smart showroom full of shiny Jaguars, Ford Granadas, and Range Rovers. He offered me two hundred quid a week and a hundred quid for every car sold, and I never looked back.

But things weren't quite as simple back in those days. Arriving on my first day in my polyester shirt and shiny loafers, my patch wasn't going to be the flash showroom but the converted petrol station over the road where they sold all the part exchanges and jalopies – a world of slightly rusty Ford Cortinas and Vauxhall Vivas. But worse was to come. Before I was let loose on a real punter, I was introduced to the art of car washing the Peter Stapleton way. A few cold, wet, and miserable hours later I'd transformed that dingy blue Volkswagen Golf into the perfect used car, and I'd learnt the first of many valuable lessons, which is that knowing how to prepare a car properly for sale is vital for the real wheeler dealer, and it's something I'll be telling you a lot more about in the coming pages.

So, I'd made it. I'd become a used-car salesman, and let me tell you I was absolutely hooked. I sold 11 cars in my first week, and the sight of Peter peeling money from a wad of notes at the end of the week was something I'll never forget. It wasn't all plain sailing, though – there were some tough times, but Peter was always there with encouragement and a reassuring word. None were tougher than when my lovely other half was hit by serious illness, and three long months later we were in big debt and I needed to do something fast. Our rescue came in the form of a four thousand pound windfall (I sold a chandelier – it's a long story) and a trip to the car auction, where I bought two cracking motors – a pearlescent white Renault 5 GT Turbo and a white Peugeot 205 GTi. Using all the car preparation skills I'd learnt at St Georges Garages (see I

told you they were important), I set about turning them into a couple of great used cars. I doubled my money and was back in business!

Don't get me wrong, I had a great time working for Budgie and the Major back in Tooting, and at Alexander Cars in Tulse Hill where I eventually ended up. From BMWs that seemed rooted to the forecourt to a Ford Cortina that wouldn't turn left, I'd seen it all. I even managed to sell the most expensive car I'd ever sold, even to this day – an absolutely beautiful Rolls-Royce Corniche convertible which I sold to none other than Phillip Green (the now-famous retail magnate) for the princely sum of one hundred and twenty seven thousand pounds! That car looked amazing, and the memories of cruising down the Kings Road with the top down and the sun shining will stay with me forever, but what I really wanted was to be my own boss, and the Renault and the Peugeot were just the start of a fantastic journey ...

As I mentioned before, I learnt some great skills back in those days – how to buy the right car, how to prepare it properly, and most importantly how to sell it. This book will tell you how to do all those things, so if you want to be a wheeler dealer just like me, keep reading!

Mike Brewer

THANKS

Getting round to writing a book has taken me ages, but I hope that what you read between these pages will inspire you to start thinking about just how much fun and how important classic cars really can be.

None of this would have been possible without the help of the following:

Thanks to my amazing writer and a man who worked tirelessly to bring this book to you, Chris Randall. Thanks also to his beautiful wife, Becky, for lending me Chris and for behaving like my second wife! Food and tea always on tap. Brilliant!

Thanks to all the photographers who have given me images to use throughout the book especially Steve Fowler (*Auto Express*) and all of the car manufacturers' PRs who have put up with my begging.

Thanks to Edd China and the team at *Wheeler Dealers* who let me indulge my passion of doing up old motors. Thanks to the team at Discovery Channel for also letting me indulge my passion of doing up old motors!

But the biggest thanks of all go to my amazing wife and daughter. They watch me walk out of the house and disappear for weeks on end while I make the shows, but are always there to welcome me back. Michelle, I wouldn't work without you. And Chloe, keep doing what you're doing – Daddy's very proud. I love you both forever.

Mike Brewer

BUYING A CAR

This is where things get exciting! You've got cash burning a hole in your pocket and you're ready to bag yourself a cracking used motor.

So where is the place to look, and what should you do when you get there? As a wheeler dealer I've bought hundreds of cars so I'm about to tell you everything you need to know. And remember, it doesn't matter whether you're buying a classic or something a bit newer, the rules are the same. Let's start at the most exciting place of all, the auction.

Buying at auction

Let me tell you, I love buying cars at auction. There's a real buzz! All those shiny motors just waiting to be snapped-up and bids flying around all over the place, but it's easy to get carried away and end up coming a cropper ... I know – I've done it loads of times myself! So where should you start? With plenty of homework, that's where.

Make sure you know exactly what car you want to buy and set yourself a budget (this is where talking to the owner's club beforehand can make all the difference) – I can't tell you how important it is get to the auction with a solid plan in your head. One of the things with buying classic cars is that values can vary a lot depending on the age, rarity and condition of a particular model, and it is only too easy to end-up paying over the odds for one of the less desirable examples. Get on the internet and find out how auctions work – there's lots of advice out there, and better still, find an auction that specialises in the sort of car you want. And don't forget the price suggested in the catalogue isn't the one you'll pay. There are other costs like a buyer's premium and tax which all add-up, and can easily take you over your budget.

Remember as well that classic car auctions can have all sorts of cars up for sale, from immaculate rare models worth mega-bucks, to barn finds that could take years to restore, and everything in between. Another important thing to remember is this – lots of people buy a classic car with the intention of restoring it, then get bored or run out of cash, or do a few bodged repairs and hope to make a bit of money. And the auction hall is the perfect place to get rid of these cars. That's why it is so important to follow my advice as the last thing you want is to get stuck with someone else's wreck!

So, you've arrived at the auction and the adrenaline is kicking in, but the best piece of advice I can give you is to take your time. Get there nice and early, find yourself a nice quiet corner, grab yourself a cuppa, and spend a bit of time going through the catalogue to narrow down your search. Once you've found a car you're interested in, go and find it in the car park and spend as much time as you can having a good old look around. Remember, this is the only chance you'll get to examine the car of your dreams so make the most of it. Give the bodywork a good going over – you want a car that's nice and straight so check all the panels, and get the trusty torch out and have a good poke around to make sure there are no horrors underneath.

And now is the time to do a few crafty wheeler dealer checks to give you a bit more peace of mind. Here they are:

◉ Take a good look at the number plates to see if there are any dealer stickers. If they are different front and back, ask yourself why. Just a replacement number plate or a bit of new bodywork after an accident? This won't always apply to classic cars but it is still a good check no matter what car you're buying.

◉ Look for a dealer name in the back window and on the tax-disc holder, as well as the number plates. These are all good clues to the car's history. Again, a classic car might not have these, but a caring owner will often preserve these sorts of bits for originality, so you might learn a bit more about the car.

⦿ And a big tip this, check all the glass to see if a registration or chassis number has been etched in. It's a simple thing but if a number is missing or different, perhaps there is something dodgy in the car's past.

⦿ Have a look at the mileage. This is often on a service sticker somewhere and might be guaranteed, but don't worry if not. There are a few things you can do to see if it's genuine, starting with the inside. You might not get a lot of time, so get a good look at the seats, steering wheel and gearlever. Another good trick is to pull out the seatbelts (if fitted!) – if they are a bit slow to reel back in, this could mean the car has had plenty of use and maybe a bit of a hard life. You might think mileage isn't so important on cars like the ones in this book, and it's true that some will have been pampered and covered just a few miles every year. However, there are plenty out there that have been to the moon and back judging by the numbers on the odometer, so it really does pay to know what to look for.

I said to take your time, and this is where that can really pay off. Don't be in a rush to get into the auction hall – hang around the car you're interested in for as long as possible. Not only will this give you a chance to see who else is interested, but you can wait for the guy who drives them into the hall. This is a great chance to hear the motor running, so have a good listen to the engine and look for any smoke from the exhaust. If the engine sounds like a bag of nails you'll know to keep the money in your pocket! Also, try to grab a word with the driver, ask him what it feels like to drive. Basically, do everything you can to find out as much as you can about the car. In the old days, there were a few unscrupulous traders around who would whip off a sparkplug lead when no one was watching so the car would run roughly – other punters would be put off and the dodgy dealer would pick up a bargain. Things have changed a bit now thank goodness – you had to be on the ball in my day – but follow my advice and you won't get caught out.

The car looks spot-on and you're ready to do some bidding. Now this part can be a bit intimidating, but relax! Look at how people are bidding so you can see how it all happens, and don't be shy. When it comes to your motor's turn in the ring, be positive and show other people that you really want it – it can put other bidders off when they see how keen you are.

When you've bought a car some auctions will give you an hour or so to return it if you find any major faults, so use this time wisely. Give the car a really good check over and test drive and, if you think there is a serious problem, or the car isn't as described, don't be afraid to take it back. This is really important with older cars so a bit of expert advice can really pay-off.

And my last bit of advice? If you're not sure about buying at an auction, take along a knowledgeable mate or member of the family to help you out.

Also, don't forget the specialist classic

car auctions – the sort you find advertised in classic car mags and at car shows and events – as you'll find loads of superb classics for sale just like the ones in this book! The thing to remember here is that they work a bit differently to the auctions I've already described. Firstly, you usually need to buy a catalogue in advance before you can do any bidding, so make sure you know the sort of car you want will be there before splashing out on the cost of the catalogue (the lots can usually be viewed online). Secondly, the cars are often on static display at the venue so you won't get the chance to see them driven into the ring like the auctions I've spent so many years at. But don't worry as you'll still get plenty of time to have a good look over the car you're after, and you can always ask the staff for help with checking that major things are working.

So, whichever sort of auction you attend, there is plenty of opportunity to grab yourself a fantastic classic motor.

Wheeler Dealer Top Tips
- ◉ Know what you want to buy and how much you want to pay
- ◉ Do your homework!
- ◉ Take your time – don't rush into buying
- ◉ Check the car as thoroughly as you can
- ◉ Be positive when bidding
- ◉ Take a knowledgeable friend

Buying from a dealer
You've decided the auction hall isn't for you, and want to head for the dealer. As a wheeler dealer I spent years on the forecourts of south London, flogging everything from rusty Rovers to beautiful Rollers, so I really have seen it all. Let me tell you what you need to do to bag yourself the perfect deal.

The first port of call is normally a trawl through the classifieds but, if like me, you enjoy poring over the small ads, things aren't always quite as they seem ... When you get on the phone, tell the seller you're ringing about the car for sale – if they say "which one?" they are probably a trader pretending to be a private seller. It's an easy trick and means you know exactly who you're dealing with.

But you've found a dealer and it looks like he's got the perfect motor for you. What's next? Well, get straight on the internet and find out everything you can about that car – make notes about the prices, the engines, the specifications, all the optional extras, everything you can find. That way, you'll have all that information in your armoury when it comes to inspecting the car, and let me tell you dealers hate it when you know more than they do! Trust me, a few hours of homework will be well worth it and you'll feel much more relaxed and in command of the deal.

Find out about the dealer too. Does he normally sell classic cars? Does he specialise in particular models? Does he have a good reputation? These are all important questions you need to ask yourself. The owner's club for the car you want might be able to advise you, or better still ask the salesman if you can get in touch with previous customers for a recommendation. A dealer who usually sells rusty old jalopies that suddenly has a classic on the forecourt probably knows nothing about those cars, so you need to be extra careful.

I always tell people they should interact with the salesman right from the off. He's there to help you buy a car, so tell him you're interested so he can grab the keys and you can get on with having a good look around. And just like at the auction, take your time! Stand back from the car and take a good look, ask lots of questions about past owners, the service history, whether it's been in an accident. Ask to look at any paperwork. Don't let the salesman hurry you – remember you're spending you're hard-earned cash, so you want to make sure you are completely happy with the car.

Now probably the most important part of any deal is the test drive, and this is where you can really get to know the car you want to buy. But before we get to that it's definitely worth trying a few examples of the model if you can – older cars can vary a lot and that way you'll know what a good one feels like to drive. The first thing I'd say is make sure you get as long a drive as possible, not just on the short route the salesman uses every day. Try to drive the car on a faster road if possible so you can really test everything properly – gearbox, brakes, the lot. Also, don't be in a hurry to jump in to the driving seat.

If the salesman wants to start by driving, that's fine – it will give you plenty of time to check the car over without having to worry about watching the road. You can listen for any noises or rattles, and push and pull every knob and button you can find! Don't be distracted by the

salesman's patter, concentrate on making sure everything works. And when it comes to your turn behind the wheel, think about whether the car feels comfortable and whether everything feels the way it should. Look out, too, for signs of 'clocking' when the mileage has been wound back to make the car seem younger than it really is. With modern digital readouts it isn't always easy to tell if any tampering has gone on, but with older cars like the modern classics in this book the chances are the mileage will be on the old-style tumblers. Make sure the numbers line-up properly and look for signs that the instrument panel has been apart. I've even come across cars with fingerprints on the inside of the glass – a big give-away if ever there was one!

Okay, so you're happy with the car and are ready to do a deal. The salesman will obviously be after the maximum profit but it's your job to get the car for the price you want to pay. So start with a low figure and work upwards – there is nothing wrong with starting with a bit of a cheeky bid, but be reasonable as the salesman does need to make a living! And remember to keep negotiations pleasant. There is never any point in falling out with the guy, and it will only end up souring the buying experience. Remember, too, that it isn't all about cash – if you can't quite reach agreement on the price, try to get other things thrown in to sweeten the deal. A new MoT, a drop of fuel, or extra warranty are all useful bargaining tools. And remember, if anything about the car or dealer doesn't feel right, walk away. There is always another car out there.

So it really is as simple as that. Follow

these easy rules and you really will enjoy buying a car from a dealer.

Wheeler Dealer Top Tips
◉ Ask lots of questions!
◉ Do your homework!
◉ Check all the paperwork
◉ Be thorough on the test drive
◉ Keep negotiations pleasant
◉ If you're not happy, walk away

Buying from a private seller

Buying a car privately can be great fun – tracking down the car you want, doing a deal with the owner – but it can be risky. You need to have your wits about you, so follow my advice to bag yourself a bargain!

The very first thing to do is to check the car's history. I can't stress how important this is – if things go badly wrong, you could be liable and lose the car and your money! It's just not worth the risk, so get a proper check done. There are quite a few companies now that can do this for you over the phone, or on the internet, and all you need is a few details like the registration number or chassis number. You might be able to get the registration number from the advert, but if not give the seller a ring and ask him for the details. If there's nothing to hide, he should be happy to hand them over and the check will tell if the car has any outstanding finance or has been written-off in an accident. Believe me, a check like this is a few quid well-spent.

When you ring the seller, don't forget the old "I'm ringing about the car" routine, just to check they aren't a trader. Now's your chance to find out everything you can

about the car – ask loads of questions about the history, the mileage, any major work that's been done, what the paintwork is like, whether everything works. A genuine seller will be happy to tell you and it will help you build a picture of the car in your mind. I hate driving miles to see a car that I know nothing about, so getting all the information first could save you a lot of time and fuel!

If you're happy with everything they've told you, now is the time to go and see the car. But don't be in a hurry to knock on the door. Have a look round the car first, and think about whether it fits its surroundings – an expensive car in a run-down area might ring alarm bells. And run your hand over the bonnet – if it's warm, perhaps the seller has run the car first to hide some faults. Be polite when you ring the doorbell and stand back a bit (if nothing else the owner might have a big dog, and I hate dogs!) – you don't want to appear aggressive in any way. And most important of all, ask lots of questions. When they show you the car, take the opportunity to ask the seller all those questions you asked on the phone – this is the perfect time to get all the information you need to make sure you're happy with the motor. Really try to engage with the seller – you'll be surprised about how much you learn about the car. Ask them whether they belong to an owner's club for that car and whether they go to shows or events. You'll find out if they are a real enthusiast – and, if they are, the chances are they've looked after the car properly and cherished it, just like you'll be doing! Ask to see the registration document so you can check the name and address match. And don't forget to ask to see any bills for work that has been done – if the owner has used a reputable specialist for that car, this is great news!

I'd always advise people to take a knowledgeable friend with them to help with the inspection, but whatever you do take your time looking over the car. Look closely at all the paintwork and the panels, checking for signs of damage or rust. And like I mentioned before, check the number plates and any window etchings to make sure everything matches. Look at the condition of the interior and make sure everything works. Check under the bonnet. Pull the dipstick out and look at the oil – does it look fresh? Open the oil filler cap too – any creamy gunge in there (we call it 'mayonnaise') could mean a blown head gasket. Does the condition match the mileage and history? Service histories are easy to fake so be on your guard. Get the engine started and look for any signs of smoke – easier if you have a friend with you, or get the seller to start the car while you check the exhaust. Blue smoke means problems, but a bit of white smoke is probably just condensation. And don't forget to look underneath the car, under the carpets and in the spare wheel well – this will help you spot any rot or chassis damage.

Now for the test drive. Don't fall for any spiel from the seller – ignore them and concentrate on driving the car. What does it feel like? Does everything work? And remember, test the car like it's meant to be driven. If it's a sports car, stretch it a bit, don't just potter around town. Make sure

it's going to suit what you want – it's too late once you've handed over the cash!

Happy with everything about the car so far? Now is the time for a bit of wheeler-dealering and, just like buying from the trade, if you fancy a bit of haggling, start low and work upwards – you'd be surprised how much you can save with a cheeky bid! But keep negotiations pleasant and check-out the seller's body language – do they seem desperate to sell? Once you've agreed on a price, make sure you're happy with the payment arrangements, and don't part with any cash until you've got the keys firmly in your hand. Don't forget, if anything worries you about the deal, walk away – there is always another car out there.

Wheeler Dealer Top Tips
- Check the history!
- Engage with the seller
- Try to enjoy the buying experience
- Make sure you are happy with the deal – if not, walk away!

Importing a car

The first thing I'd say is don't be afraid to do this. I've imported loads of cars in my time – from Europe and the US – and it's easier than you think as long as you do your homework in advance! With the internet, it is easier than ever to find that special classic in another country – get yourself a cheap flight and hotel and you could pick up a bargain!

But the really important thing to remember is don't get carried away. When you find the motor you've always wanted you still need to do all the checks that I talk about in this book. Here are the things you'll need to know:

◉ Be very wary of doing a deal without seeing the car. Those shiny pictures might not be all they seem, so I can't stress enough how important it is to go and see the car for yourself. You might enjoy a fantastic holiday at the same time!

◉ Remember to factor-in the extra costs. I don't mean just the travel – there will be shipping and storage costs and you will probably have to pay things like taxes and VAT when the car lands in Blighty. You'll also have to register the car and get it tested so It really pays to find out before you take the plunge.

◉ Find yourself a reputable shipping agent. Places like the US have simply thousands of businesses that can sort out shipping, but ask owner's clubs if they can recommend someone.

◉ Make sure all the necessary insurance and other paperwork is in order before you start.

◉ Take plenty of photos of the car before it gets shipped. I know plenty of people who have found bits missing from their treasured car when it reaches the UK (sadly this really does happen) so pictures will mean you have proof of its condition.

◉ Don't forget that you'll need to arrange for the car to be transported from the UK port to wherever you live. You probably won't be able to drive it away as it won't be registered, so bear this in mind.

If all this sounds a bit daunting, don't be put-off. There is plenty of advice out there to make sure everything goes smoothly, and the UK's government websites can tell you everything you need to know about the paperwork and any taxes.

Importing a car can be a real adventure and a fantastic way to start your classic car ownership. Go on, give it a try!

Wheeler Dealer Top Tips

◉ Avoid buying a car unseen if at all possible

◉ Do your homework and find out about the paperwork and costs in advance

◉ Only use a reputable shipping agent for your new pride and joy!

OWNERSHIP

So you've bought the car of your dreams, now you need to look after it and perhaps do some work on it too! So what's the first thing you need to do? Get in touch with the owner's club, that's what!

I know I say it a lot in this book, but clubs really are a fantastic source of information and advice on the best specialists, and remember that lots of the cars in this book have huge on-line communities dedicated to that particular model.

The internet has really changed things for the classic car owner and I really recommend joining in – you'll be amazed at the expertise and information that's out there, and you'd be mad not to take advantage of that (and you could make some great new friends too). If you've just bought something a bit special you want to keep it that way!

But before we get to any of that, there are a few things I want to say about owning a modern classic. And the most important thing to remember is something I tell everyone who asks about these cars, which is that you should see yourself as the guardian of that car. What do I mean by that? Well, my whole wheeler dealer philosophy when it comes to classics is that we are only looking after them for future generations to enjoy. That means lavishing as much time and attention on that car as you can, and trying to do every job to the highest standard you can afford. Classic cars need plenty of TLC – remember that and running one of these cars will be a real pleasure. Whatever you do don't be tempted to bodge work as it will only come back to bite you later, and you'll just be spoiling a wonderful classic motor!

Also, get to understand the car you've bought. Find out everything you can about it, really get to know the car and the costs involved in doing any work. Now we're all on the internet, there is just so much information there is no excuse – make yourself an absolute expert on your motor and I guarantee you'll enjoy the ownership experience a lot more.

And the last thing before I get to the information you really want to know is ... be prepared for the inevitable. You're driving a classic! It's like driving around in a grandfather clock – old and precious, just like me! So expect it to break down sometimes. But don't worry about that – just enjoy the whole ownership experience – and join the AA!

Now to the work stuff. I've got the great Edd China to look after my cars but as you probably won't have him in your garage, here are my top tips for getting the very best from your cherished motor.

The oily bits
Engine

◉ Make sure you service the car regularly. Sounds obvious doesn't it? But it's surprising how many owners let the maintenance slip, particularly if the car isn't used that much. There is so much information available to help you look after your car, so there really is no excuse for not knowing what needs to be changed and when. It also helps you to spot small problems before they become big ones – and ending up with an even bigger bill!

◉ Shop around for parts. Dealer and specialist prices can vary a lot, even for exactly the same part, so it pays to check first. A little time spent on the phone or internet can save you an awful lot of cash!

◉ If you think a particular job is too difficult, find a specialist to do it for you. I really can't recommend enough the importance of finding good local expertise, and the owner's club is often an excellent source of advice for finding the best people in your area. Go and introduce yourself, get to know "Terry from the tyre shop" – they will be much better than the big names who are just after your money, and these local lads will really care for your car. Building up a good relationship with them will help you no end when it comes to sorting any problems.

◉ Try to re-use parts where possible. Not only will this save you money, but metal bits like rocker covers and air cleaner housings can often be cleaned-up and resprayed. It's easy to do at home and just takes a bit of elbow grease to keep your car looking nice and original.

◉ Don't forget that bits like carburettors and alternators can usually be rebuilt using kits available from dealers and specialists. New replacements are often hugely expensive, so have a go at refurbishing instead. It isn't as hard as you think and a bit of time and patience can really save you cash.

◉ Don't be afraid to upgrade your car. Just about every classic out there has some weak spots and cures are often available in the form of remanufactured and upgraded parts. For example, if a weak cooling system is a common problem in your car, why not consider fitting a better radiator – you'll be amazed at what's available and again the owner's club can give you advice. While I always try to keep cars original wherever possible, there is nothing wrong with making improvements that will make your motor better to own and drive.

Gearbox and transmission

◉ Replacing a gearbox or differential on a classic can be a seriously expensive business, so don't rush into anything. Remember, it's important to get a proper diagnosis before you start changing parts, so get an expert to take a look if necessary. That seemingly disastrous oil leak could be cured by just fitting a new seal or gasket somewhere, so it might not be as bad as you think.

◉ If the whole unit has gone kaput, then consider getting the original rebuilt or fitting a reconditioned item. Brand new parts will really give your wallet a pounding so do a bit of homework first and see what's available.

Steering, brakes, and suspension

◉ The first thing to remember is these are safety-related items, so whatever you do don't be tempted to cut corners!

◉ Always use good quality parts. Items like reconditioned steering racks and boxes are fine and are a lot cheaper than new ones, but only buy from a reputable source. Again, your local mechanic or specialist is a great source of advice.

◉ Don't forget to consider upgrading. More modern brakes and suspension parts make a lot of sense, and lots of companies produce items that improve on weak or poorly designed originals.

Wheels and tyres

◉ Wheels that are looking a bit tatty can easily be refurbished and make all the difference to the look of the car. There are plenty of companies offering this service so find out who the owner's club or forums recommend. It often costs less than a hundred pounds per wheel, much cheaper than buying new ones assuming they are still available.

◉ Consider replacing aftermarket wheels with the original design. Personally, I reckon this always looks better, and you can buy them from specialists or the internet. You can always part-exchange or sell the aftermarket ones to help offset the cost.

◉ Keep a close eye on the tyres. If you're car only covers a few miles a year (even though you should be out driving it as much as possible) it is easy to forget about them and they will degrade over time. This is where your local supplier really comes in handy as they can help you find the best deal. But don't skimp here – why spoil your lovely classic with cheap tyres, and you want it to be as safe as possible.

The interior

◉ Keep the interior nice and clean, and consider using something like Scotchguard® on the carpets and upholstery as it will help protect them from dirt and any accidental spillages. You might even want to consider a professional valet every now and again. It might cost a few quid, but it'll be worth it. Remember it's all about protecting the resale value of the car. While I'm on the subject of the interior, try not to mess with it like cutting holes for speakers and the like, unless you've got spare trim to return it to original condition.

◉ The internet is a fantastic source of new and replacement parts like seat covers and carpets and just about everything is available. Remember though that a good

clean might be all that's necessary to bring back that original showroom look.

◉ Repairing upholstery and trim can be a tricky business though, and often needs a bit of skill to get that perfect look. I'm not saying don't tackle it yourself, but consider using a specialist trimmer for any tricky jobs. You'll be amazed at what they can do to bring tatty seats and woodwork back to life and the cost is normally pretty reasonable compared to buying new parts. And it all helps to keep that lovely original look.

◉ I've recommended a few convertibles in this book, and this is another area where using a specialist can be a good idea. If it just needs a clean-up, there are plenty of products on the market that can liven up a tired hood. More serious wear and tear might mean a replacement is needed and this is where costs can soon mount up, particularly if you want a genuine replacement part. I know I keep saying it, but check out the specialists and websites. Classic car magazines are full of companies selling good quality pattern parts, and while you might need a bit of help with fitting, you can save an absolute fortune.

The bodywork

◉ The first thing I always tell people is to keep the car clean. Not only does it make the car look great, it gives you a great chance to examine the bodywork properly and spot any damage or rot before they cause serious problems.

◉ Use a really good quality polish to protect the paintwork – there are lots of good brands out there and, trust me, it really makes a difference. And if it does look a bit faded, don't worry as you'll be amazed at what modern products can do to help you recapture that showroom shine. The professionals use a term called "mopping" (MOP means Machine Operated Polisher) which basically means using a rotary polisher to really remove all that grime and faded paint. You can hire everything you need for a reasonable amount so it's definitely something to have a go at yourself.

◉ Repairing accident damage or rust properly is probably one of the hardest jobs to do on a car, and takes a lot of skill to get right. By all means have a go yourself, but if you're not confident get a professional to do the job for you. Trust me, nothing ruins a classic car more than bodged bodywork, and any potential buyers will run a mile!

◉ If you fancy doing the job yourself, only use good quality replacement panels. That doesn't have to mean expensive originals – there are plenty of pattern parts out there but bad ones won't fit properly and you'll end up with a terrible result. It really isn't worth the risk.

◉ If the car is in need of a total respray, then this is probably another job for the professionals. But it's vital that you get a top quality job, so try to get some recommendations from other owners or clubs. You can save yourself some money though by doing the preparation work. This really pushes up the cost of any work so removing trim and other parts, and rubbing down panels ready for painting can save a fortune.

◉ Remember that items like exterior trim and lights aren't always available new for older cars, so be extra careful when removing them. Consider refurbishing old parts or sourcing replacements from specialists or the internet.

◉ Everyone assumes that any plastic parts like bumpers and grilles need to be replaced if they are damaged, but that isn't always the case. Replacing something like a bumper on a modern classic can run into hundreds of pounds when you include preparation and painting, but repairs are often possible. It's definitely worth checking with owner's clubs and forums for advice – you'll be amazed at what's possible.

◉ The most important thing when it comes to protecting the bodywork of your classic is to store it properly, especially in winter. If you can keep it in a garage, that's perfect, but don't forget to air the garage and the car regularly. In fact, you know what – using the car is better than storage. Show it off at events and shows. Don't lock it away – if it's cheap to run and insure, get the benefit from it and get out there and drive!

VISIT VELOCE ON THE WEB – WWW.VELOCE.CO.UK
All current books • New book news • Special offers • Gift vouchers • Forum

CHAPTER 3

SELLING A CAR

Knowing how to prepare a car might not seem very important but believe me it is, as I found out on my very first day in the motor trade all those years ago.

I spent literally hours washing that old blue Golf until it was absolutely perfect, and it taught me how to make a used motor look its absolute best – vital when it comes to getting the best price. It doesn't matter how much work you've done to a car, if it doesn't look the business when a buyer comes to see it you're already in danger of losing the sale, and that's not what being a wheeler dealer is all about!

Preparing a car for sale

It never ceases to amaze me how little effort people make when it comes to tidying up their cars, and believe me I've seen some real shockers – an interior full of old crisp packets and with overflowing ashtrays is never going to tempt a buyer.

If you've read the chapter on ownership (what am I saying?, of course you have!), then you will have kept your cherished motor in top condition, but I'm going to give you some reminders anyway.

All it takes is some time and effort to turn a dowdy old motor into something fit for the showroom, and here's how:

◉ First of all, get yourself the right equipment. Just a few pounds spent at an accessory shop will get you everything you need then you're ready to make a start.

◉ Cleaning the outside sounds easy, but there are a few things you can do to make it look as good as possible. Firstly, don't forget to do all those areas that are normally hidden away. Open the doors, bonnet, and boot and clean all the areas you can see – it's no good looking shiny on the outside if it looks grubby as soon as the buyer opens anything. And, if the car has got a spare wheel, take it out and clean the well it sits in – it's little things like this that show a buyer the car has been cared for.

◉ Now the car is sparkling, it's a good time to have a look at the bodywork and see if there are any little bits that need attention. Touch in any stone-chips, replace cracked number plates and look for any small dents or scratches. There are companies out there that can repair small areas of damage for relatively little cost

and they can come to you to do the work. I guarantee it will be worth it.

◉ Finally, with everything else done, give the paintwork a good polish as the finishing touch. Use a decent quality polish too – now isn't the time for cutting corners! And don't forget the chrome and wheels as well.

◉ Give the interior the once over. Is everything looking as smart as it can be? Use upholstery cleaner on the seats and carpets to brighten things up, and if your car has got lovely leather seats treat them to some hide food. Nothing puts a buyer off more than a grubby and uncared for cabin, so spend plenty of time and effort in here.

◉ Get under the bonnet and check that everything is okay. If it's looking a bit grimy, get the engine steam cleaned, and don't forget to clean all the painted areas like the inner wings and lock panel. And lastly, check all the fluid levels and make sure everything is up to the mark.

Remember, this is all about making the right impression with potential buyers and showing that you have really cared for your car. And because you're the guardian of a wonderful classic I know you'll have looked after it properly! I've already talked a lot about buying a car, but selling is just as important. You want to get the best price you can, so it really pays to do your homework before sticking an ad in the classifieds.

How to sell a car

The first thing to think about is setting the price. Start by seeing what others are charging for similar cars, so you can get the asking price spot-on. It only takes a little bit of time spent on the internet to see what's out there, and it will help you attract buyers. You can save yourself a lot of hassle by asking friends or family if they want to buy the car, but whoever you sell it to don't be bullied into letting it go too cheaply. If you're not happy with the price that's offered, wait for another buyer!

If you do decide to advertise the car, prepare it properly. Make sure buyers can see that you've cared for it – it really does make all the difference. When it comes to the advert, spend some time writing a good description. You know the car better than anyone, so make the ad interesting and a bit more personal. You want your treasured motor to stand out in a sea of other adverts so don't rush this part. And take some great pictures, make the car the star! Using a good location for the pictures will really help as I guarantee that seeing your car surrounded by rusty prams and scooters won't help it sell! And don't be afraid to include pictures of any slight damage or corrosion – buyers will appreciate your honesty and will know what to expect when they come to view. Make the photos as high a resolution as possible and ensure you are happy with how they look – grainy or blurred pictures are very off-putting!

Have a think as well about the best place to advertise the car. There are lots of classic car websites and magazines out there, and you'll be advertising your motor to the right sort of buyer. There might even be an enthusiast magazine for your type of car, so this is a great option. And don't forget the owner's club – they might know of a buyer waiting for just the right car, and it could be yours!

Get all the paperwork together including the receipts for any work. People like to see that you've spent money on the car. Keep everything handy so you can answer questions on the phone and, most importantly, be honest. Don't try to hide anything about the car as you'll just end up with annoyed buyers. When someone comes round to view the car, tell them as much about the car and your time with it as possible – trust me, people like to hear this stuff and some interesting background could help you make the sale. If you belong to the owner's club or take the car to shows and events, for goodness sake tell them about it. If you've got any pictures of the car at a show, that's even better – the buyer will see that you are a real enthusiast and they'll feel much more comfortable buying the car from you.

And, most importantly, make sure the money is in order. Never accept personal cheques, just cash or a banker's draft, and never hand over the car until the money is safely in your account!

Wheeler Dealer Top Tips

◉ Do your homework and set a proper price for the car

◉ Get the car ready for sale – a car that has been cared for will sell more easily

◉ Spend the time writing an interesting advert, and take plenty of good pictures

◉ Have all the paperwork in order ready for when the buyers call

◉ Don't release the car until you have the money!

FAMILY/STARTER CLASSICS

If you're just about to take the plunge into the world of classic motoring, my advice is to keep it nice and simple. It is so easy to come a cropper when you're dealing with old cars, so why make life difficult for yourself by buying something complicated and expensive?

Much better instead to start with something fun and simple, and that's why this chapter is about those starter classics. There are simply loads of cars out there that won't cost you a packet to buy and run, but will still give you plenty of enjoyment. Here are my favourites.

Avoid rusty ones and this could be the perfect starter classic.

Ford Escort MkI

I absolutely love a classic Ford – there are just so many fantastic cars to choose from and my dad, who was a famous car-customiser back in his day, loved his Fords too. I remember him owning the superb Zephyr, and me learning to change gear in his Transit van! But one of my favourites is the Escort.

My brother Terry had an Escort, so I reckon that's where my enthusiasm for these came from (we had some great times in that car I can tell you) but I was still

Want something a bit sportier? The Twin Cam is spot-on.

25

a cute three-year old when it hit the UK market in 1967!

The Escort became one of the biggest sellers of the decade. It replaced the successful Anglia and was fitted with the tough 'Kent' engine which would go on to be used in a whole load of cars over the years. It even introduced rack and pinion steering to Ford's family cars, a big development back then. But Ford didn't forget the performance fans, and the Escort range included the 1300GT fitted with a twin-cam Lotus cylinder head, and the epic Mexico. Not only was the Mexico a true fast Ford, it achieved plenty of success on the rally stage too in the hands of Roger Clark. The highlight was winning the 1970 London to Mexico rally with Hannu Mikkola (one of my all-time rallying heroes) at the wheel, sealing its reputation as a true classic!

The Escort range continued to sell

Just look at that colour scheme. That says rallying to me!

when I was well into my twenties (okay, early thirties if I want to feel old!) and I sold loads over the years. In fact I reckon I must have sold 10% of all the Escorts made – well it felt like it anyway – and the car was a real friend to me helping to pay more than a few bills.

In my mind this is one of the perfect starter classics. Still relatively cheap and there are plenty of them around to choose from so there is no reason not to bag a good one. And I reckon they've aged well, much like myself! Lots of families had one of these so it might bring back a few memories too. Having said that, you still need to be careful as they do have their faults.

Avoid the dealers who will be asking lots of money and, instead, head for the classifieds where you'll find lots for sale, most of them in decent nick. The first thing I tell everyone when looking at Escorts is to buy one that is as original as possible. There is a big market in historic rally cars – the Escort was really successful in its day – so many have been turned into fake Mexicos, and lots will have been tuned and then thrashed to within an inch of their lives! Instead, look at spending five grand or more and you'll find a car that's been looked after but might still need a bit of work. Perfect for the budding wheeler dealer!

If there is one thing that does for these Escorts, it's rust and my goodness do they rust! So, you'll need to take plenty of time to check a potential purchase. The first place you should look at is the inner wings and the top of the front suspension turrets from inside the engine compartment – I've seen plenty looking a bit ragged in these areas and a proper repair can be pretty costly. Another place they go is around the A-pillars and front door hinges, so if you don't want the door coming off in your hand have a proper dig around here for signs of rot.

I'll be saying this a lot in these chapters, but get underneath and have a really good look at the floor and chassis. I know from experience how easy it is to get carried away by a shiny exterior, only to forget that all that polish could be hiding horrors underneath. And repairs here can be tricky and really damage your wallet.

Lastly, watch out for cars that have a vinyl roof. These were popular options on cars of this era but can hide a multitude of sins – if you spot any signs of bubbling under the vinyl it could easily be rust taking hold, and you should probably walk away.

There's better news on the interiors though. They are very simple and parts are generally easy to get and quite cheap. So if it is looking a bit tatty inside don't worry too much – getting seats retrimmed and new carpets fitted is pretty straightforward and shouldn't cost a fortune either.

The one thing to check, though, is the dashboard. These are prone to cracking after years of sitting in the sun and replacements are scarce. It's not the end of the world but a tricky job that can be avoided if you buy the right car.

You really don't want an interior that's been hacked about by boy racers fitting big speakers and the like. As I said at the beginning, originality is the key with these cars.

And the really good news is that the

mechanicals are nice and simple. There is nothing complicated under the bonnet of an Escort so there is no need to panic if a bit of work needs doing.

The engines were tried and tested and are really easy to work on. A simple toolkit will be enough for most jobs and just about every mechanic cut his teeth on engines like these. Parts are plentiful and cheap and even a complete rebuild is well within the scope of the amateur. And if you fancy a bit of tuning, there are loads of parts out there to give you a bit more power. To be honest, the same can be said about the rest of the drivetrain so as long as the car has seen regular maintenance there really shouldn't be much to worry about.

A good long test drive will show up any major problems, so if there is anything, you'll be able to haggle!

The perfect starter classic? Pretty much!

Nice looking and easy to own, the Viva is hard to beat.

◉ Mike recommends

A 1972 Escort Mexico in that wonderful bright orange. If you find one, let me know as I want one!

Vauxhall Viva HB

Don't fancy the Escort? Then how about something a bit different, the excellent Vauxhall Viva. This is another car that I remember my dad owning, and he had a great taste in motors – must be where I get it from! He used to drop me off at school in the Viva and I thought it was brilliant even back then.

Probably not the first car that springs to mind I know, but the Viva really does make sense if you are looking for a simple and enjoyable classic. Between 1966 and 1970, over half a million HBs were produced and introduced us Brits to the 'coke-bottle' styling that would be copied by car makers for years to come; most famously by Ford with the Mk3 Cortina. Okay so the 1.1-litre engine was a bit weedy, but the 1.6- and 2.0-litre units that followed had enough go, and the Deluxe model even threw in a heater and carpets!

If you wanted a bit more fun, there was the 79bhp 'Brabham' edition (yes, Vauxhall really did advertise 79bhp as a plus point!) – incredibly rare and sought after now – or the more readily available Viva GT with its Rostyle wheels, white paintwork and black bonnet. Pretty cool I reckon.

The Viva is another one of those cars that lots of people remember having in the family and, on the whole, were driven by more sensible owners so are unlikely to have been thrashed or abused. Another benefit of choosing a Viva is that they have a good following in the classics community with a lively owner's club and social scene.

It might only have 79bhp but worth it for those sidestripes alone!

But just like the Escort, there are things to look out for so let's start with the bodywork and the dreaded rust. This was always the Achilles heel of British cars back in the 1960s and 1970s, so time spent checking now could save a lot of pain and expense later, trust me.

From inside the engine compartment the first places to check are the inner front wings, the bulkhead between the engine bay and passenger compartment and around the battery tray. The Viva had a nasty habit of rotting in these areas and repairs can be both tricky and expensive –

if the car you're looking at has already had work done here, its excellent news.

The rear wheelarches are another weak point, and you must have a good dig around in the boot and the spare wheel well as well. Rear damper mounts got pretty flaky so check these too. Blocked drainage holes can rot the bottoms of the doors and the sills, and, as always, make sure the floor is straight and rot-free. If all these areas look good, you're probably well on the way to bagging yourself a tidy motor.

Interiors are nice and simple too, and, to be honest, pretty basic. But that's good

Looks basic now but this was sporty back in its day.

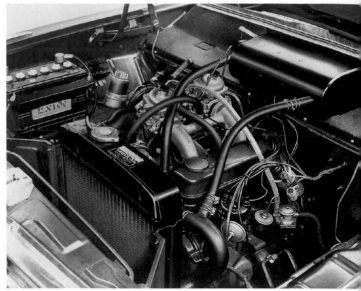

Easy to look after and twin carbs too – good for a bit of extra power.

news for you as there isn't too much to go wrong and any problems should be obvious. An important thing to bear in mind is that trim and other bits and pieces are a bit rarer than with other cars, so it really pays to get a car with an interior in fundamentally good condition.

Seats and carpets that need a bit of attention aren't a big problem – there are loads of specialists out there that can do the work – but items like door cards may not be so easy to source. And if the headlining or dashboard are damaged, you are probably better off getting back to the classifieds and finding another car. The message here is buy the best you can afford.

Another thing these cars have in common with the Escort is nice, simple mechanicals. There is nothing under the bonnet to frighten the novice and as long as the previous owner has kept up the servicing, there shouldn't be anything to worry about. All engines could leak a bit of oil but, as long as it's not excessive, new gaskets should cure the problem. And, if any work does need doing, parts are plentiful and every back street mechanic will be able to do the job. The 4-speed manual gearbox was tough but I'd avoid the automatic. The Borg Warner auto 'box was reliable but sapped what little power the Viva had, and it wasn't much fun to drive.

Lastly, if you do fancy a GT watch out for fakes. A set of wheels bought on the internet and a hand-painted bonnet tempted a few dodgy sellers. Do your homework and you'll know exactly what you're getting.

Mike Recommends

A 1600 SL in silver, or a nice original GT. The choice is yours.

Iconic car, great colour. You must own one of these in your lifetime!

Mini

Ben Hur wasn't the only long-running classic to be launched in 1959 because that was the year when we first saw the truly iconic Mini (I'm not sure which lasted longer to be honest!)

Designed by the brilliant Alec Issigonis the Mini changed the face of family motoring forever. With front-wheel drive and a transverse engine under its stubby bonnet, the Mini allowed room for four in a car just ten feet long – a true packaging miracle! And, what's even better, is that it comes with a superb motorsport pedigree having won the Monte Carlo rally back in the '60s with Paddy Hopkirk and other great drivers at the wheel.

This really is one of my all-time favourite cars and is completely classless. From students to stars, everyone loved the Mini and there were plenty of celebrity owners back in the swinging '60s who wanted to be seen whizzing around London in this legendary little car. Peter Sellers, Twiggy, the Beatles – they all had a Mini. And listen to this – even Enzo Ferrari had one! It really is the coolest of small cars. And, of course, it is still going now in the hands of BMW, though it looks a bit different to the ones I remember!

The original Mini is just such great fun to drive and it handles like a go-kart – if there is one car you must own in your lifetime this is it.

Really old ones, the Mk1 with the external door hinges, are getting rare now so I wouldn't look for one of these. Go for a bog-standard Mini 1000 or, preferably, a 1275GT for even more fun.

But superb as they are, the Mini does have a reputation for poor quality so I can't stress enough the importance of doing your homework and checking any potential purchase really carefully. There are just so many of these cars around to buy, that there really isn't any excuse for landing yourself with a duff one.

As always rust is the thing to look for. It's a notorious problem with these cars. The first thing I always tell people is to start at the front and look for any signs of rot around the headlamps and edges of the front wings. Even if it doesn't look too bad, rust could easily have spread to the inner wings and replacing a whole front end starts to get expensive. It's such a problem in fact that you can even buy a whole glass-fibre front for a Mini – bonnet and all – and while it's not exactly original it does avoid a lot of future problems.

The sills and floor are another area to check – I know quite a few owners that have jacked-up the car to change a flat tyre and the jack has gone straight through the floor! Don't say you haven't been warned ...

Another area you absolutely must look at is the boot floor. In a Mini the battery is in the boot, and the battery tray rots-out – having the battery drop straight through the floor onto the road is no joke, believe me!

Check the A-pillars around the door hinges (have a good look from inside the car) and the bottoms of the doors too. Have a good look at the roof gutters, too, as these rot.

Check the mountings for the front and rear subframes as well as the subframes themselves. These subframes are fairly cheap and easy to replace though, and most Minis have had a few new ones in their lifetime.

If all this sounds like bad news, don't be put off. The good news is that absolutely everything is available for the Mini including whole new bodyshells, but a rot-free example really is the holy grail when looking to buy a classic Mini.

Interiors are nice and simple and there isn't much to go wrong. Early cars had a speedometer and steering wheel and that was about it! All parts are available from specialists and there is plenty of opportunity to make the interior of your car a bit more special if you fancy it. Fit a small steering wheel and a cheap bracket to lower the steering column, and you really have got a great little go-kart.

The trusty A-series engine is a real gem and an absolute piece of cake to repair. Just about every car enthusiast has worked on one of these at some time or another, and a decent set of modern tools makes any job pretty straightforward. Just check for any signs of overheating, blown head gaskets and oil leaks. In a clever piece of design, the gearbox was mounted below the engine and, while basically sound, can suffer from worn synchromesh on first, second and reverse gears. Any crunching on the test drive will give the game away. And don't worry about the chattering noise from the gearbox at low

The Mini interior couldn't be simpler and you'll feel like Paddy Hopkirk!

speeds – this is just the idler gear and is all part of the Mini character!

And with even more innovative engineering there was a clever suspension system too. Some models were fitted with compact rubber cone suspension (known as the 'dry' system) while others got the fluid-filled Hydrolastic set-up (known as the 'wet' system). Both gave the Mini terrifically agile handling, but the dry system is easier to work on and easy and cheap to replace.

The 1275GT is definitely one of my favourites. With a nippy 59bhp and lovely 'Rostyle' wheels, it replaced the classic 998cc Cooper. The only downside for me is that it was based on the flat-fronted Clubman bodyshell which I never liked that much, but it's a small price to pay for so much fun! The 1275GT was also way

ahead of its time, offering an early version of the run-flat tyre with the Dunlop Denovo system. Mind you it wasn't that popular at the time so don't bet on finding one fitted with these now.

Tuning has always been a big part of the Mini-owning scene, so if you fancy a bit more style and performance there are loads of parts out there to choose from and plenty of advice available. Give it a try and you could end up with something really special.

I really can't recommend a Mini highly enough. Do all the checks I've told you about and the Mini you buy will give you the most fun you've had in a car, I guarantee it!

○ Mike recommends

A nice original 1275GT in red. Superb!

CHAPTER 5

HOT HATCHBACKS

Everyone who loved cars back in the 1980s will have hankered after a hot hatch and, believe me, I was one of those people. Great performance wrapped in a practical hatchback body was a fantastic combination, and when VW launched the iconic Golf GTI, every car maker wanted a piece of the action. Which is great news for those wanting a good value classic as there are still lots of hot hatches around on the used market.

I've owned and driven loads of these cars over the years, and here are my absolute favourites.

Ford Fiesta XR2

Let me take you back to 1981 when Ford launched the MkI XR2. They took a car from the supermarket-run and turned it into a hot hatch, and every teenager wanted one! With a trusty twin-choke Weber carburettor Ford squeezed 84bhp from the 1600cc 'Valencia' engine, enough to hit 60mph in 9.3 seconds.

Just a few grand will bag a decent XR2, they are fun and easy to own, and there is a big fan club for help and advice. And they are so nippy to drive. Okay, performance is slow by today's standards but they were simple cars that offered a pure driving experience, with none of the equipment and safety gear you get today. Find a nice original car and put the fun back into your motoring!

The fact these are such simple cars means checking a used one is easy as long as you keep your wits about you. A British car of this age means only one thing. Rust! So you need to check all the usual places including the wheelarches, the bottoms of the doors, the sills, the front suspension turrets and inner wings, and the tailgate.

The good news is that replacement panels are cheap and any decent body shop can do the job at a reasonable cost. There wasn't much in the way of special parts on the XR2 but items like spoilers are hard to find now, and you'll be looking at second-hand bits if anything does need replacing. Owner's clubs will be able to help here though.

The engine in the XR2 couldn't be simpler, which makes it perfect for the DIY-er. Get yourself a decent set of tools

The classic '80s hot hatch, and I just love those wheels.

and there probably isn't any job you can't tackle. And if you don't fancy having a go yourself, every mechanic will be able to work on them. They don't suffer from many problems either. Thrashed ones will get a bit smoky, and the tappets will start to make a racket without regular adjustment. Head gaskets go, but this is an easy fix, and watch for oil leaks from the sump and rocker-cover gasket.

Personally I'd avoid tuned ones – the original has plenty of character and this is a car you want to keep nice and simple. Hard use will put a strain on the clutch and gearbox, but both are regular Ford parts and replacement isn't too costly. All the other mechanical bits are straightforward and easy to replace, but the special 'Sonic' alloys corrode easily. Refurbishment is cheap though at about fifty pounds a corner, so get rid of any aftermarket replacements – the originals look best.

The car's weakest point is probably the interior. Quality wasn't brilliant when the XR2 was new and time will have taken its toll. Collapsing seats and cracked dashboards are common, but avoid any cars where previous owners have cut holes in the trim for big stereos and speakers. Some bits are getting hard to find now so originality really is the key here.

Just a few grand will bag you a really nice example, and the Ford club scene will introduce you to a whole new world of mates!

◎ Mike recommends

A nice original car, with the correct alloys.

Peugeot 205 GTi

The 205 GTi was already selling well, but on a mission to stay ahead of its competitors Peugeot upped its game again in 1986 with the launch of the even better 1.9-litre engine. The all-aluminium XU9 motor was fitted with the latest Bosch L-Jetronic injection system for an impressive 130bhp. With disc brakes all round, vented at the front, the little Pug could stop as well as it went and, trust me, it really went! Sixty came up in a scorching 7.9 secs and it would hit 130mph flat-out – seriously impressive back then. Extra kit like half-leather trim and electric windows as standard sweetened the deal even more.

With the 1.9 engine, the 205 really was the hottest of hot hatchbacks, and my favourite without a doubt. I reckon it's even better than the Golf GTI when it comes to the driving experience as you just feel so connected to the road. Short gearing meant punchy performance, and with

The best hot hatch ever? I reckon it could be ...

stunning grip it was simply awesome from A to B. It would show up many modern cars that's for sure. It was light too, which helped the performance and handling no end. With all of today's safety regulations, we probably won't see a car like this again so grab one while you can!

The 205 is a great ownership proposition, but there are some faults you need to watch out for. That lively handling got inexperienced drivers into trouble so many got accident-damaged – I really recommend a history check on these to make sure there are no horror stories lurking in its past. A thorough inspection will give you peace of mind too. I always look under the bonnet and in the boot to make sure the inner wings and floor are ripple-free, and a check of the floorpan is a good idea as well. Check the rear suspension mounts and the front bulkhead too, as these are weak areas and tricky to repair. If the car has gone into a ditch, this is where it will show.

Although rot isn't that common, body panels were pretty thin, so rust bubbles in the doors, sills, tailgate and wheelarches are things to watch out for and could be a sign of poor accident repair. Take a good look around the seals for the front and rear

The 205 has a great driving position and those seats are seriously comfortable.

screens for any signs of bubbling, as this can be a fiddly and costly repair.

Faded paintwork and peeling lacquer are common issues so a car that hasn't been looked after could well be ready for a respray. A lot of these cars will also have damaged or faded plastic trim and, while you can normally bring this back to life with a bit of elbow grease, some parts are scarce so bear that in mind if the car you are looking at is tatty.

Despite a reputation for unreliability, the engine in the 205 is actually pretty tough, though it is safe to assume that most will have been thrashed. A bit of noise from the valve gear is normal, but a smoky exhaust isn't, so a rebuild won't be far away. Evidence of careful and regular maintenance is a must-have with these cars.

The biggest issue was poor running caused by faulty airflow meters. I can remember selling these cars when every single one we had seemed to have the same problem. I got pretty good at

swapping units from showroom cars to keep a customer happy! If the engine stalls on the test drive, then the airflow meter is almost certainly the culprit – new replacements are hard to come by but there are specialists out there that can rebuild them at a reasonable cost.

The electrics can be a bit flaky too, so watch for any warning lights that don't go out. Tracing the cause can cost plenty in labour so bargain hard. The gearchange was fantastic on the 205 when it was new, so if it feels loose or it jumps out of gear, replacing the linkage with new parts usually sorts the problem. Weak synchromesh on third and fourth gears was a bit of an issue as well but reconditioned 'boxes aren't a fortune if the worst happens.

That awesome handling relied on properly sorted suspension, so make sure everything is healthy in this department. Any signs of uneven tyre wear means something is amiss, and if the car doesn't feel sharp on the test drive or there are any clunks or groans from underneath, then budget for a rebuild. Front suspension

That cracking 1.9-litre motor is good for 130bhp.

bushes wear quickly with hard use, and the rear axle beam bearings can seize-up if a problem is ignored – a replacement is around £800 and a few hours' labour to fit.

The 205 was also popular with the tuning brigade, and a few even had turbos fitted. Companies like Turbo Technics did some quality conversions but a thrashed one will be expensive to put right. Lowered suspension, and engine swaps from other Peugeots (the 2.0-litre unit from the 405 Mi16 was a popular choice) are common too, but I reckon you should stay away from these and get a nice original example instead.

If I had to pick a weak point, then I'd say it was the interior. They felt flimsy even when they were new, so worn seats and tatty carpets are common. The sporty seats are really comfortable but the side bolsters get a bit threadbare, while the cheap carpets seemed to attract dirt and oily marks like a magnet!

There's a big market in new and second-hand parts for these cars though, so refreshing a tired cabin won't cost a fortune. The one thing you do want to avoid is a cracked or damaged facia. Replacements are hard to come by and a fiddly job to do, so try to find one in good nick if you can.

Spend 5-6k on a nice example and I guarantee you will have one of the most fun cars ever made. A truly brilliant hot hatch.

○ Mike recommends

A last-of-the-line 1992 1.9 with ABS and power steering, in that gorgeous 'Miami' blue.

The car that started it all, the wonderful Golf GTI.

Volkswagen Golf GTI MkI

The car that launched dozens of imitators, and started the hot hatch craze. With a few tweaks and a more powerful engine, VW suddenly had a hit on its hands and has never looked back.

That classy Guigiaro-shape arrived in the UK in 1979 with a fuel-injected 1600cc engine, but it's the later 112bhp 1.8 that you should be looking for. Reliable and with superb engineering, there is almost no better hot hatch to own and without all the gadgets and safety kit of today's motors, gives you a really pure driving experience. And thanks to that German quality, there are still plenty of cars on the market today so finding a good one couldn't be easier. With regular maintenance, the Golf GTI really is almost bullet-proof.

They can be prone to a bit of rust though, so I always check around the slam panel, the chassis legs under the bonnet, and the inner front wings. The bottoms of the doors, the sills, and the boot floor and spare wheel well should come in for attention too. The good news is that there

Performance and hatchback practicality. Perfect!

are plenty of good pattern parts available, so a bit of bodywork shouldn't be a deal-breaker if the rest of the car is sound. Strangely, the brakes weren't the Golf's strongest point due to a complicated linkage in the conversion to right-hand drive, so quite a few got crashed by owners not used to the extra performance – make sure you're happy that everything is nice and straight.

That 1.8 engine was strong and good for high-mileages with regular maintenance, though faults with the Bosch K-Jetronic injection systems can cause rough running. An enthusiastic previous owner should have kept things up to scratch, but keep an eye out for blue smoke on start-up, leaking head gaskets and oil leaks. These aren't difficult engines to work on though, and every part is available, so don't be afraid to tackle maintenance yourself. As always, a big folder of bills and service history is what you're looking for.

The rest of the mechanical bits are reliable, and a decent test drive will show up any problems. One thing you really want to look for is an original set of alloy wheels (I reckon the Pirelli-pattern ones are particularly cool) – they are cheap to refurbish and aftermarket wheels really spoil the look. If they are missing, lower your bid accordingly and track down a set on the internet. They make all the difference to the stylish GTI. 'Campaign' and 'Pirelli' editions are sought after now so you might have to pay a bit extra for these, but avoid cars with tasteless body kits – they were all the rage back then but I reckon they spoil the pure lines of the original. Watch out for fakes too – it's easy to stick GTI bits on a boring GL model, so don't get caught out!

One of the best things about the Golf GTI was the interior. The stripey seats and golfball gear knob were pure '80s, and solid build quality ensured they lasted well too. Originality really is the key with these cars, so if the interior has been damaged or messed about with, then I'd be walking away. A nice original car will be an absolute pleasure to own and this is what you should be looking for.

Lastly, VWs have a fantastic fan base and club scene so get yourself a lovely GTI and you'll make plenty of new friends!

⊙ Mike recommends

A nice original 1.8 in silver. Pure 1980s hot hatch fun.

A bodykit and BBS alloys. Now that's '80s style.

The Golf GTI is at home on the road and the track.

Solid build and those lovely tartan seats make for a great interior.

It wouldn't be a Golf GTI without that gearknob.

I reckon black really suits the terrific Type-R.

Honda Civic Type-R

Japanese car makers were never that good at hot hatchbacks – I still remember the dreary Sunny and Almera GTIs – until Honda hit on a winning formula with the terrific Type-R. Now this was a seriously hot hatch with a 197bhp 2.0-litre VTEC engine that revved to 8000rpm and could punch the Civic to 60mph in around 6.5 seconds and on to nearly 150mph. Now that's what I call performance!

I love these cars – not only do they go like a rocket but they really handle too, and they are brilliant fun on your favourite road. This second generation car is my favourite model – pick up one of these and you'll never have so much fun for so little cash.

Introduced in 2001, even the early ones are still quite new (trust me, they will definitely be a future classic) so expect the car you're looking at to be in good condition. If it's not, it means the previous owner has neglected it and you should be getting straight back to the classifieds to find another one. There are loads for sale out there so be fussy!

That neat shape with its subtle spoilers looks fantastic, and there isn't that much to look for either. The first thing I always tell someone looking for one of these is to get a history check done. The last thing you want is a car that's been stolen or crashed, so don't take any risks with the sporty Civic.

There weren't many colours to choose from when they were new, but I reckon black or silver look best – just take a good round the bodywork to check for dents, stone chips, or any signs of accident repairs. A few have been given the lowered suspension and privacy glass treatment, but I reckon you should avoid these. A pampered original car is what you should be after.

The Typo R is all about that fantastic, high-revving VTEC engine, and you really do need to make sure everything is healthy under the bonnet. The good news is that there are no cambelts to

41

worry about as the valve timing is by more reliable chain. Having said that, proper servicing is everything with this car as that 2.0-litre engine is quite highly stressed, and that means regular oil changes. Any neglect in this department can lead to poor oil pressure which can affect the chain tensioner and the VTEC variable valve timing system, so make sure you see a fully stamped service book. I'd definitely avoid any cars with tuned engines and big exhausts – they've probably been thrashed (the Type-R is a favourite at track days) and a replacement engine isn't cheap! Gearboxes and clutches can take a pounding (another reason to avoid 'chipped' examples) so make sure everything feels healthy on the test drive.

That unusual dash-mounted gearlever with its wonderful alloy gear knob should slot smoothly into gear. Watch out for clunks from worn suspension bushes, tired brakes, and kerbed alloys. Amongst the things I love about these cars is that the steering and handling are just so sharp and they feel fantastic to drive, so if the car you're looking out doesn't feel like this there is definitely something wrong and it's time to walk away.

The Type-R had a lovely sporty cabin which should still be in excellent condition. Seat bolsters can wear on high-milers and the odd rattle from the dashboard and trim isn't uncommon, but there shouldn't be anything major to worry about. As with all the cars in this book, the condition of the interior will tell you a lot about how the car has been treated, so check carefully and make sure everything works. Find one with

A cabin built to last, but that alloy gearknob gets a bit chilly in winter!

The 2.0-litre VTEC motor delivers nearly 200bhp, and it loves to rev!

air-conditioning if you can – this was a popular option and well worth having.

So, if you're looking for a reliable and exciting hot hatchback, look no further than the superb Civic Type-R. I love it and so will you!

◉ Mike recommends

An unmodified car in black or silver with air-con. Fantastic hot hatch fun!

CHAPTER 6

CLASSIC CONVERTIBLES

For lots of people – me included – the combination of a modern classic and a convertible top is just about the perfect mix. I reckon you really can't beat driving through the English countryside in a superb motor feeling the wind and sun on your face and, let's face it, the rain too!

That's why I couldn't do this book without mentioning some of my favourite drop-tops, and the good news is that all of them can be picked up for reasonable money. Grab one of these for the summer and you won't regret it.

My brother loved these terrific cars, and you will too.

Triumph Spitfire

I'm going to use that phrase again, but this really is another of those classless cars. It doesn't matter whether you're a student or an RAF pilot, you'll just love the fun that the Spitfire has to offer. This is just about the perfect starter convertible.

With its lovely styling by Italian designer Michelotti, I was still a twinkle in my dad's eye when the Spitfire hit the road in 1962 with a simple 1147cc engine, basic interior and a chassis and suspension based on the popular Triumph Herald. The Spitfire was developed over the years with bigger engines and more power, but the one I love the most is the 1500 model available from 1974 until the end of production in 1980. Around 95,000 were built, and with twin SU carburettors and 71bhp, it was capable of the magic 100mph. My brother Brian always

hankered after this wonderful car but could never afford one, but he'd have absolutely loved it, and so will you.

Now I know British cars from this period didn't have a great reputation, but don't be put off. There are still lots of good Spitfires around and if you follow my advice, you'll be able to bag a good one.

Number one on the list is the chassis. If there is anything you need to check before handing over the cash, this is it! Rust is a big enemy but, before you get underneath, there is a very simple test you can do. Grab a pound coin and check the gap between the door and the rear wing – slide the coin into the gap at the top, and then the gap at the bottom. It should be the same. If it isn't then there is a good chance the chassis is broken, and you should most definitely walk away!

If everything seems okay, now is the time to have a good dig around under the

The Spitfire looks great from any angle – what a wonderful little roadster.

car and make sure the floor or sills aren't rotten. Most cars out there will probably have been repaired already, but if not it's a fiddly job that can be avoided if you check carefully. While you're under there, check for damage to the chassis or exhaust system – the Spitfire sat close to the road and speed humps can give the underside a pounding.

Have a good look in the boot, too, as this is another area where rot occurs, and don't forget to check around the rear bulkhead, where the fuel tank is mounted, as this is a known weak point. The large bonnet/wing section is a dirt trap so make sure rust hasn't taken hold there. And one last thing you can do to check the car hasn't seen some accident damage: lift the bonnet and, using a tape measure, check the length of the chassis rails either side of the engine. Both sides should be exactly

the same – if they aren't, I'd be going back to the classifieds to find myself another car!

Interiors are nice and simple but if it's looking a bit sorry for itself, don't worry too much. There is a huge following for these cars and loads of specialists out there that can supply every nut, bolt and screw. So if the rest of the car is straight, sorting a tatty interior isn't a difficult or expensive job. It is worth checking under the carpets, if you can, just to be sure that water leaks haven't allowed rust to take hold in the floor.

An unloved interior could mean the previous owner hasn't looked after the rest of the car either, so be extra careful when you're checking it over. While we're talking about interiors, get a good look at the hood too. This was never brilliant, even when new, but if it's torn or damaged,

A bit of wood on the dash and a cosy cockpit – just superb.

These engines are so easy to work on and you get great access too.

budget for a replacement in the asking price – again, good specialists can supply everything you need.

Mechanically, the Spitfire is pretty reliable, but the best news is that any work on the engine is a piece of cake. Why? Because the whole front end of the car lifts up for access – bonnet, front wings, the lot. My Edd tells me that removing the bonnet is simple and makes everything nice and easy to reach.

Overheating and blown head gaskets are issues on the Spitfire so check carefully for these – any signs of oil in the coolant or a creamy emulsion under the oil filler cap is bad news so, if you want the car, make sure the price comes down accordingly. General wear to the cylinder bores and crankshaft are also common so watch carefully for any blue smoke from the exhaust. If you do buy one of these cars, my tip is to replace the standard radiator with a larger core version – it improves the cooling no end and helps to avoid future problems.

A good long test drive will show up any problems with the rest of the drivetrain. Gearboxes and differentials can get a bit rumbly with age, but specialists can supply reconditioned units for a reasonable price. Some gearboxes came fitted with an 'overdrive' unit as well, operated by a switch on the gearlever. It's worth checking this works as sorting a failed one can be tricky and there are plenty of cars where the owner hasn't bothered. The engine revs should drop almost instantly when you flick the switch if everything is healthy.

I really can't recommend this superb British classic enough. Wind in the hair motoring has never been so much fun and that's why I love the Spitfire so much.

⊙ Mike recommends

A well looked after 1500 in bright yellow or period French blue. Avoid the cheap ones and buy the best you can afford. Remember, a broken chassis is a disaster!

A really classy convertible, and I reckon that colour suits it too.

Not all convertibles look good with the hood up, but this one does.

BMW 3 Series (E30)

The E30 hit the road in 1982 with a range of four cylinder engines, but it was 1986 when the wonderfully silky 170bhp straight-six was introduced as the 325i. No doubt about it, this is the best engine and the one I would look for.

Classy, aspirational, great German engineering and a superb rear wheel drive chassis. Who wouldn't want one of these! BMW has always had a fantastic reputation for producing high quality cars that are also great to drive. Every single car has sporting DNA running right through it, and the 3 Series is no different. Combine that with gorgeous looks and you have just about the ideal classic convertible. I absolutely love these cars, and I think you will too!

But this is a car where you really need to have your wits about you when buying. Check out the classified ads: there are absolutely loads of E30s for sale, ranging from the pampered to abused wrecks. The first thing I say to anyone after one of these motors is to avoid modified cars. For

some reason, they are really popular with the aftermarket brigade and you can hardly move for cars with fat alloys and lowered suspension! Body kits can trap dirt too and lead to rot.

Get a nice original car that's been looked after, and make sure you do a history check – the one thing you don't want with an E30 is a car that's been crashed or stolen! Crashing wasn't uncommon either as all that power, and tricky handling in the wet, caught drivers out and sent many a 325 to the body shop.

Even the latest examples will be getting on a bit now, so check the bodywork carefully. For all their BMW quality, rust can be an issue so look in all the usual places – the bottoms of the doors, the sills, the rear wheelarches, the valance below the rear bumper, and around the windscreen.

Take a good look at the paintwork – the factory paint was a top quality job so a proper respray will cost plenty. And don't even think about buying one of these without making sure the hood is in

Sporty and solidly built, BMW makes some of the best cabins around and this one's no exception.

That gorgeously silky straight-six. This is the engine to go for, no doubt about it.

top condition! I've seen so many where the hood is torn and creased and a good quality replacement is seriously expensive. If it looks good on the outside, make sure it works properly too – an electric top was a popular option but it's a complex mechanism and it will cost an arm and a leg to put right! If the owner will let you, get the hood up and put the car through a car wash – it really is a great test and will help you spot any weak points or leaks.

Interiors were pretty robust on the E30 and a car that's been looked after should still look good today. You can expect a bit of wear and tear, but damage to the seats or dashboard should ring alarm bells – there are plenty of specialists out there that can supply parts for these cars, but replacing trim isn't cheap so avoid anything too battered. Again, something nice and original is what you want. Press every button and switch you can find to make sure everything works. Faulty electrics and weak air-con are surprisingly common so budget accordingly.

As I mentioned before, the 6-cylinder engine is my pick and you are looking for a car with acres of service history. Although fundamentally strong and good for mega mileages if looked after, cracked cylinder heads, leaking head gaskets and worn valve gear are weak points. Smokiness and oil leaks aren't unheard of either, so don't rush any checks, and make sure the car has had regular cambelt changes.

Weak synchromesh on manuals, jerky automatics, and whining differentials are things to watch for too. That good long test drive that I'm always telling you about will show up any problems though.

Lastly, quite a few of these cars got clocked so make sure the mileage matches the condition. And keep an eye out for the service indicator in the dashboard which used a system of lights to tell the owner when a service was due – when the green lights went out it was time for a garage visit. But aftermarket resetting tools could be bought cheaply so you want to be sure that any servicing really has been done.

If all this makes the Beemer sound like a bit of a risky motor, don't worry. If you do your homework and check it carefully, I guarantee you will end up with one of the best looking, best engineered convertibles out there. And my last bit of advice? Avoid the really cheap stuff, and instead spend 6-7k on a nice example.

◯ Mike recommends

A 1998 325i in Dolphin grey with those gorgeous BBS alloy wheels. Simply fantastic!

Mazda MX-5 MkI

This is simply one of my all-time favourite convertibles – the most reliable, clever

The MX-5 looks fantastic, but just make sure you avoid the rusty ones.

A perfect driving position and slick controls makes this a great place to be.

two-seater in the world. It was spot-on from day one, and if MG had its time again it would have done the brilliant MX-5. Mix Japanese reliability with go-kart handling and you've got yourself a perfect modern classic. And the good news is that there are simply loads to choose from on the used market so finding a good MkI model is easy. England might have been doing badly in the World Cup (as usual) but there was much better news in 1990 because that's when we first got the lovely little MX-5. With a revvy 1.6 twin-cam engine (a more powerful 1.8 came later) and double wishbone suspension, it proved an instant hit with buyers.

Rust does get to these cars, though, so it pays to be thorough with the inspection. The sills (particularly at the rear where it forms part of the rear panel) and rear wheelarches are common places to find rot, but if there is one area you absolutely must check it's around the windscreen, A-pillars, and front wings. Bubbles under the paint around the windscreen seal is a sure sign that things aren't right, and repairing this properly is a really time-consuming and fiddly job – just ask my Edd!

The paintwork tends to fade too, and a difference in colour between the plastic nosecone and the bodywork is common. Expect early cars (which only came in red, blue, or white) to be ready for a respray.

The revvy twin-cam engine is virtually bullet-proof but make sure it's been regularly serviced.

Watch out for crash damage too, and do a history check. A poor repair could mean the body is twisted and if that happens, it will never be right.

The soft-top was really simple and could be raised or lowered without even leaving the driver's seat, but it pays to have a good look at the condition. The plastic rear screen had a tendency to crack, and while later ones had a glass screen this could mean the hood itself cracking instead – not good news. Replacements aren't too costly but again budget for this when making a bid. And a bit of advice that applies to all convertibles – be wary if the hood is down when you go

to inspect the car. It might seem obvious but there are unscrupulous vendors out there that hope you won't check and you only find out the hood leaks like a sieve when you get the car home! Make sure you see it up and working.

Interiors are nice and simple which is good news. There isn't a lot to go wrong, so just make sure all the knobs and switches work and, if the worst happens there are lots of specialists out there that can supply new or upgraded parts for the little Mazda. Make sure you try the pop-up headlamps though as motors can fail. The only other thing to watch out for is damp and mouldy interiors. Leaking hoods and

Styled on the classic Minilite wheel, these alloys really suit the little drop-top.

seals will soon lead to a stinky interior, and the only answer is to replace the upholstery and carpets. If you see an old MX-5 being driven with the hood down, the owner is probably just trying to get rid of the smell!

With proper servicing, the lively little twin-cam engine is virtually bullet-proof. A fat sheaf of bills for any work done is what you want to see, including ones showing regular cambelt changes (though a snapped belt shouldn't cause the pistons and valves to meet, so it isn't a disaster).

MX5s can suffer from the odd oil leak from the cam cover too, but it's not a serious problem. Gearboxes are equally tough, and the gearchange should be like a rifle-bolt. If it isn't, something is amiss and replacement 'boxes are costly, so make sure it feels good on the test drive. And check the clutch feels right as well, as slave cylinders are known to fail.

Suspension bushes will wear at high mileages and ruin that superb handling, but replacements are fairly cheap. Bear in mind, too, that early cars weren't fitted with power steering, though with such wonderful feedback on the road, I wouldn't worry about this. Lastly, if the original 14-inch alloys are fitted (which I reckon really suit the car), check for kerbing or corrosion.

I'd always recommend you avoid the really cheap cars. Spend upwards of 3k and even a ten-year-old motor should feel like new. One thing people always ask me is whether they should avoid the imported Eunos models, and my answer is always a resounding 'No.' The scare stories around these are mostly rubbish and as long as the proper changes have been made to make them UK-legal, there shouldn't be anything to worry about. The only thing you might find is that original radios won't tune properly in the UK so you could be stuck on Radio 4, but it's an easy fix.

I reckon the MX-5 really is the perfect convertible classic so what are you waiting for?

⊙ Mike recommends

A pampered original car in black. Bright colours look good too, so take your pick. A real pleasure to drive and own.

Just look at that stylish bodywork. This has got to be one of the best-looking cars on the road.

VW Karmann Ghia Convertible

Elsewhere in this book I've already mentioned that the VW Beetle is one of my all-time favourite classics, and here's another Vee-Dub that has something in common with it. Let me introduce you to the absolutely stunning Karmann Ghia. Based on a Beetle chassis but with bodywork designed by Ghia in Turin, I reckon these are one of the best looking cars on the road. Built by Karmann, this is Italian style with German engineering – a brilliant combination!

Built between 1955 and 1974, over 400,000 of these cars rolled off the

Osnabrück production line with just over 80,000 examples being this lovely convertible. 1959 saw the introduction of right-hand drive ragtops, and the good news is that there are still plenty around in the classifieds so bagging yourself a bit of style should be nice and easy.

But as with all old cars, there is plenty to look out for with these, starting of course with the dreaded rust. If there is one thing I need to tell you about the Karmann Ghia, it's that rot can strike just about anywhere, so you really need to have your wits about you when you're inspecting a car. You need to go over all the panels with a fine-tooth comb, and make sure you get a good look at the floorpan, sills and the floor of the front luggage compartment. All of these areas can rot away leaving you with nothing but a big hole and an empty wallet!

The good news is that replacement panels are still available but the bills will soon mount up if extensive bodywork is needed. Tired paintwork is likely to be found on neglected examples so budget for a quality re-spray if things are looking a bit tatty. If possible, think about importing a LHD car from the US – many have lived their lives in dry conditions and don't usually suffer from the rust problems we get in damp old Blighty!

Engines and gearboxes are pretty much standard VW air-cooled stuff, which means parts and expertise are plentiful, and there is plenty of scope for some tuning if you fancy a bit more performance. My Edd absolutely loves these engines and I know there are lots of go-faster bits available to make your car really special. Mind you, although they might be simple, don't forget to do some basic checks. Oil leaks from the engine and gearbox are a common problem and might have done damage if they've been ignored. Rotten heat exchangers and fuel systems can cause problems too, and watch out on the test drive for cars that jump out of gear as it means a reconditioned gearbox or rebuild is on the cards.

Steering, brakes and suspension are all nice and simple and, as long as the previous owner has kept up the maintenance, shouldn't give any problems. Worn bushes or seized joints are the main things to watch for, and a

Nothing complicated in here, but watch for signs of water damage from leaking hoods.

good long test drive should soon show up any issues.

Interiors are nice and simple with little to go wrong, so there isn't much excuse for buying a tatty example unless you really want a restoration project. I've seen some really nasty cabins in these cars, but a caring owner should have kept things nice and tidy. It's worth checking for any signs of water leaks that might have damaged the carpets or trim, and don't forget to check the condition of the hood.

You can buy everything you need for these cars so sprucing-up a tired interior is easy and not too expensive. I really recommend you join the owner's club for these cars as they are a fantastic source of advice and support and will really help you get the best out of the fantastic Karmann Ghia.

⦿ Mike recommends

A 1500 in a lovely bright colour. LHD or RHD, it doesn't matter – you'll love it either way!

You too can pretend to be Bobby Ewing in the gorgeous SL.

Mercedes SL (R107)

If you were one of the millions of people watching 'Dallas' back in the early '80s (and yep, I admit I was one of them), then you'll have seen Bobby Ewing driving around in the gorgeous Mercedes SL. The SL is the perfect combination of style and solid German engineering and is definitely one of my all-time favourite cars. And it's

a car that has been around for a while too, the first of these models were launched in 1971. But it's the later cars that I love the most and I reckon a late '80s model is pretty much perfect.

One reason for going for a later car is that the rust-proofing was much better. Surprisingly the SL has a bit of a reputation for rot, so unless you are

The build quality is rock solid but make sure everything works in here.

prepared to pay top dollar for one of the mint cars on classic car dealer forecourts, then it pays to spend plenty of time checking a potential purchase.

Rust can bubble up on the tops of the front wings, in the rear wheelarches, and in the sills. These areas are relatively easy to repair – at a cost – but corrosion can also attack the windscreen surround, the bulkhead between the engine bay and cabin, and the boot floor. Sorting these out is a much bigger job and I'd

A great convertible and a gorgeous colour, the SL is just lovely.

be walking away from any car that has problems here.

Remember, the SL is a top quality motor and any repairs on the body or paintwork need to be perfect to avoid ruining this wonderful classic, and that could have a disastrous effect on your wallet! So avoid wrecks at all costs!

Another thing to bear in mind is that lots of these cars were treated to the 'skirts and spoilers' look and some of these mods can be pretty tasteless. Go for it if you like that sort of thing, but make sure the extra bits aren't hiding any rot. Beware of chrome wheelarch embellishers: they can hide a multitude of sins!

The engines in these cars are simply superb. Although the straight-six is smooth and refined, I'd definitely be looking for one of the characterful V8s. They might be a bit thirsty but you'll forget all about that the minute you put your foot down – great performance and that wonderful burble from the exhaust will be all you need to convince you. And they are tough units too. A quarter of a million miles is possible with regular oil changes, but they aren't without some faults. Smoky exhausts, leaking head gaskets, worn timing chains, and fuel injection problems are things to watch out for on neglected cars and rebuilding or replacing a tired engine is seriously expensive. You definitely want to see evidence of regular maintenance to put your mind at rest.

Most SLs came with a smooth and strong automatic gearbox, and these are the ones to go for as they really suit the character of this German cruiser. A decent test drive will show up any problems, so if it's jerky or reluctant to change gear some expensive work will be needed. Avoid the rare manuals – the gearchange was notchy and unpleasant and ruins the car for me.

Items like suspension and brakes are strong and reliable and shouldn't give problems if the car has been maintained properly. Keep an eye out for corroded alloy wheels, though refurbishment isn't too pricey.

The interior of a well looked after SL is a lovely place to be. Mercedes build quality was rock solid in those days and as long as you do a few checks, the cabin should be comfortable for years to come. The first place to start is to look for any signs of water leaks and a check of the carpets and footwells will reveal any damp. Leaking hood seals could be to blame, but leaks can be notoriously hard to cure so be wary of problems here.

Make sure everything works, as bringing items like air-conditioning and electric windows back to life can get expensive. Check that convertible hood properly too, making sure it operates smoothly – a quality replacement is hugely expensive ...

Most SLs came with a separate hard top so make sure this is in good nick and that the mounting points on the body aren't damaged. And here's a good tip. If the car you're looking at has got the hard top fitted, ask the seller if they will remove it (it's a two person job really) so you can check the condition of the convertible hood. Unscrupulous vendors will hope you don't ask and could be hiding a hood that is in terrible condition, or even missing altogether! Trust me, I've seen this happen!

It might seem like there are lots of things to check with the SL, but, believe me, it will be worth it. Find a good one and I guarantee you will have bagged one of the coolest and best engineered convertibles on the market.

○ Mike recommends

A 500SL with that wonderful V8 engine. Red or navy blue are my favourite colours on these.

It has just got to be the all-white model for that real feel of the '80s!

VW Golf GTI Convertible

I know I've already talked about the hatchback GTI but I absolutely couldn't resist including the stylish convertible. If you spent any time in the posher parts of south west London back in the eighties (I did, and you don't need to be so surprised!) you could barely move for these trendy soft-tops. The 'Sloane Rangers' loved them and it's easy to see why. Not only did you get the great performance and solid engineering of the iconic hot hatch, but you could enjoy the wind in your hair at the same time. What a terrific combination!

If you've already read about the hatch, then you'll know the things to look out for with these cars. Find a 1989/90 example and rot shouldn't be too much of an issue, though it pays to check all the same. I don't know why, but for some reason the convertibles tended to be better looked after than the hatchbacks, but a look at the door bottoms, sills, and rear wheelarches will confirm that everything is healthy. A good look underneath is advisable too, just to make sure that damp carpets haven't allowed rust to take hold in the floorpan.

Mechanically these convertibles are the same as the hatch so the same issues apply and, as always, a big folder of servicing bills will put your mind at rest: so look for a car that has been well maintained. Plenty of owners wanted the convertible for more relaxed motoring so quite a few were fitted with an automatic transmission – it wasn't the smoothest unit when new and, personally, I prefer the manual 'box, but the test drive will reveal anything untoward. Worth bearing in mind is that VW also sold a lower-powered version of the convertible badged as the 'Clipper' which came with a carburettor version of the 1.8 engine, so make sure the seller isn't trying to pass this off as a genuine GTI.

Being a convertible, there are a few extra things to check before you hand over any cash. As always, you need to check the interior for any signs of water leaks – the GTI had a good quality hood so leaks are likely to be caused by damage to the fabric or seals. Replacement hoods are available from specialists at a reasonable cost, but factor this in when it comes to the asking price. Make sure the mechanism operates smoothly too – replacing the fabric is one thing but repairing or replacing the frame will add serious costs to the job. Also fading or cracking of the trim and dash can be caused by lots of time in hot sun with the roof down (not that likely in the UK I know) and replacements parts are getting scarce.

Probably one of the most popular models was the all-white edition – paintwork, hood, seats, alloys, everything was white. I reckon these look pretty good but the interior can soon look grubby if it's not cared for properly. Budget for a full valet if the car you're looking at has a tired cabin.

And that's pretty much it for these. The GTI is stylish, well-engineered, and probably one of the coolest convertibles on the market. What more do you need from a modern classic?

⊙ Mike recommends

A nice original car in full-on '80s white. Lovely!

CHAPTER 7

MIKE BREWER'S THE WHEELER DEALER KNOW HOW!

TALES FROM THE TRADE

I've had some fantastic times as a car dealer, and those days back in south London were some of the most fun I've ever had. Together with my ever-patient wife Michelle, I've had plenty of highs, but also a few lows, which show that even an expert wheeler dealer like me sometimes gets it wrong ...

Take for example the lovely 1989 Astra GTE that I had prepped and ready for sale. A lovely motor and the phone didn't stop ringing. First to come and see it was a young Italian guy called Pedro, an MoT inspector as it turned out. He arrived up at my house in south London straight from work and still in his oily overalls.

Well this guy spent hours looking over the car – he checked the tyres, in the boot, under the bonnet, underneath the car, absolutely everywhere. If anyone knew what to look for it was this guy. He starts it up, has a listen then turns it off for another look round. So now he's ready for a test drive, so in he gets, adjusts the seats and mirrors (he's a short guy), turns the key ... and nothing. Dead as a door nail! He jumps out and spends ages looking under the bonnet and wiggling wires but to no avail. By this time, he's been at the house for about three hours and drunk all my coffee and Mrs B has lost patience. So we send him packing, but we've still got a dead car. Time to call the AA which reckons it's a faulty ECU (having spent ages looking for it, the guy finally finds it hidden in the footwell and establishes that it's a Bosch unit), and trailers the car to the nearest Bosch service centre. They agree with him, but a new one is seriously expensive – I can see my profit disappearing over the horizon – so I'm straight on the phone to every scrap yard I can find to track down another one.

I strike lucky in Cambridge, which is miles from where I live, so I enlist the help of my brother, Terry, to give me a lift. The place is awful – ankle deep in oil and with a terrifying Alsatian dog on a chain – but they've got the ECU. The bad news is they want £500 for it. No choice but to hand over the cash, I give the ECU to Terry who promptly stumbles over an old bit of car on the ground and drops it! As you can imagine I was fuming and didn't speak to him for the whole journey home. And does it work when we get it to the service centre? No! But a day later the Bosch guys give me a call to say the car is running and I am overjoyed. But it wasn't the ECU at all. It was an immobiliser switch hidden under the driver's seat that Pedro had activated when he moved the seat ...

So, what with the new part and the labour bill, I'm about a thousand pounds out of pocket, but a new buyer from Luton could be the answer *if* I can deliver the car to him (strangely enough this buyer was an auto-electrician who found the whole Pedro-saga very funny, but I'd lost my sense of humour by then). Not a problem and a chance for Terry to redeem himself, so off we set round the M25 – me in the Astra, Terry in a Honda Shuttle I also had for sale. Everything is going fine until I notice the temperature gauge heading for the red so it's over to the hard shoulder for some head-scratching.

With a bone-dry cooling system and not a drop of water to be found I even contemplated having a pee into the radiator, but neither of us wanted to go! And then a brainwave hits me when I realise I can use the water from the Honda's windscreen washer reservoir. So in it goes and we set off again, and it's only a mile or so before I notice what looks like foam bubbles in the rear view mirror. In no time at all, me and the Astra are completely engulfed in huge clouds of bubbles and with other motorists pointing and laughing; it's only then I realise that it's the windscreen washer fluid being foamed-up in the Astra's radiator. A quick stop at a motorway service area (surrounded by more laughing drivers – I've never felt such an idiot in my life!) means I can get plenty of clean water in and finally deliver the car to Luton. All this for a £500 loss! If only the new owners had known what I'd been through ...

And it wasn't always my own cars either. Dropping in on a car dealer friend that I used to trade cars to, Michelle and I found ourselves being asked to hand over a car to a buyer. My friend had some business to attend to and asked if we'd deal with the paperwork on a Nissan Prairie – the car was all ready to go, so all we had to do was get the lady who was buying the car to sign the paperwork, hand over the money and that would be it.

But my mate (who I can't name to save any embarrassment) made it very clear that I was to make sure she signed the warranty document. And I soon found out why. The hand-over went smoothly and the lady drove away very happy, but it was only when my mate returned that he explained that the reverse gear on the car didn't work. It doesn't matter

he said because when she comes back to complain I'll get it paid for under the warranty. And you know what? She never did come back, so I guess she never reversed anywhere. It's a strange business, the car game!

But this one was my fault. I'd just paid £4000 for a V8 3-door Land Rover Discovery, in white, and I was convinced it would sell as everyone loved the Disco at that time. But not this one they didn't.

It sat on my forecourt for a whole six months and I never had a sniff of a buyer in that time. But one day the phone rang and it was a posh-sounding guy who said he'd definitely buy the car if I could deliver it to a field out in the countryside. I couldn't wait to get rid of the Landie so I agreed and spent a couple of hours sitting in the field absolutely certain that someone was winding me up.

All of a sudden, I hear the sound of a helicopter which lands in the field and out steps Jonathan Palmer – ex-Formula 1 driver and a doctor to boot! He wanted the Discovery as a course car for his track day business and handed over the money there and then. Not all good news as I lost a thousand pounds on that motor, but I'd certainly learnt a lesson about buying white 4x4s!

1. *A budding wheeler dealer! I loved cars even at that age.*

2. *I even flogged the odd scooter ...*

3. *I helped set up one of the biggest 4x4 dealerships in the country.*

4. *Sales meetings were all part of the job!*

5. *An immaculate showroom just waiting for the customers ...*

6. *Where all the deals were done!*

7. *Another happy customer!*

⑧ *This one is finished and ready to earn some profit.*

⑨ *I told you the 3 Series is one of my favourite cars. Definitely money to be made with this one.*

⑩ *Mrs B, her mum, and her beloved 7 Series BMW.*

⑪ *Even Mrs B was roped into preparing the cars for sale.*

⑫ *My favourite view of Mrs B!*

13 *Almost done and then it's onto the forecourt.*

14 *The Daytona is gorgeous, not so sure about the shirt!*

15 *You just can't beat a bright orange Escort Mexico. Lovely!*

16 *It's all about the preparation and plenty of elbow grease.*

17 *You don't see many around but the stylish Datsun still looks good today, much like myself!*

18 More French style with the classy Citroën SM.

19 With another of my favourite cars, the lovely BMW 2002.

20 A bit of profit. That's what I like to see!

21 Another of my favourite classics, the lovely Volvo P1800.

22 An old car and a workshop, the perfect place to be!

23 Just where I love to be – the driving seat of a luxury motor.

24 Getting up close and personal in the bodyshop.

CHAPTER 8

MIKE BREWER'S THE WHEELER DEALER KNOW HOW!

LUXURY CLASSICS

Don't fancy something sporty? Well how about a bit of comfort? I've got some great ideas for travelling in luxury for not much money. The great thing about this group of cars is that they depreciated like mad when they were new, so now you can pick up a real bargain. And you really do get lots of car for your cash. There is nothing like a classy classic to make every journey special, and my favourites are true luxury motors.

Bentley Turbo R

You must think I'm mad picking a Bentley, but trust me they can be picked up for so little money now. The Turbo R is a true gentleman's express for real drivers, and I've got a real soft spot for them. This is craftsmanship in the best tradition, a superbly engineered car from what I reckon to be Bentley's best era.

Not only do you get all that luxury, but a car that can outperform hot hatches too. What a combination! And you know the funny thing, the Turbo R reminds me of Ray Winstone – thoroughly British but packing a real punch!

First hitting the road in 1985, early cars were fitted with Solex carburettors to pump fuel into that massive V8. Bentley were always cagey about publishing power outputs, but the later Motronic-injected cars had around 328bhp, and I'd recommend going for one of these for their reliability and smoother running, and the ability to hit sixty miles an hour in an amazing 6.7 seconds. The thing to remember is that the Turbo R was seriously expensive when new, with running costs to match, so you really do need to do your homework and buy carefully to avoid a costly nightmare. But it can be done!

Bodywork should be in immaculate condition, even on the oldest examples. Rust can start to nibble away at the doors, wings, sills, and boot lid and good quality repairs will cost a fortune. If it looks like the car has been repaired, quiz the previous owner carefully to make sure the work is up to scratch – you don't want anything that has been bodged. The same goes for the paintwork and I'd avoid any issues

If you can't find a nice Turbo R, a Brooklands will do very nicely

here at all costs. The preparation time for a good respray runs into many hours and it will cost loads. You really do want the best condition you can find. And, while you're at it, take a good look at all the brightwork like the bumpers and grille. They can be repaired, but again it's an expensive job. And while I'm on the subject of bodywork, avoid white cars unless you're thinking about dabbling in the wedding market!

The interior of a Turbo R is gorgeous and really charming with acres of wood and leather, and it should still be in good condition today. Every material used was of the highest quality so if it is looking tatty, it's a sure sign of a careless owner and I'd advise finding another car. There are plenty of skilled specialists out there that can refurbish the interior, but it will come at a cost and a big one at that! The wood veneers were specially matched for each car, so repairs are for experts only.

There are plenty of toys to play with too, and just about everything that moves has an electric motor, so check everything

Full of wood and leather, this is what owning one of these cars is all about. Sheer British class!

so find yourself a reputable specialist and enjoy everything this wonderful engine has to offer. Just watch for oil leaks and any signs of overheating.

Even with only three-speeds, the automatic gearbox was very smooth – if it isn't, consider finding another car. Power steering pumps didn't last long, and any noises or notchiness at the steering wheel means impending failure. Reconditioned ones are a cheap replacement though.

That magic carpet ride quality was partly down to a complex rear suspension system, and there are plenty of joints and bushes to wear out and give trouble. Have a good listen on the test drive for clunks and rattles from the rear of the car.

Good examples of this car are getting rare now, so find one now and enjoy some real British luxury.

⊙ Mike recommends

A pampered car in metallic blue with grey leather interior.

It might be complex and thirsty but the V12 is one of the truly great engines.

74

SPORTING CLASSICS

This is where things get exciting when it comes to the world of modern classics. There are just so many fantastic cars out there that I really struggled to decide on my favourites. The best bit of advice here is to really do your homework and spend some time talking to specialists before you take the plunge.

You could be spending quite a lot of cash and it's all too easy to come a cropper when you see that gorgeous supercar sitting in front of you. Get it right though and you'll have bagged yourself something really special.

I've owned one of these and I just love the styling.

Volvo P1800

I've sometimes imagined myself as that suave English detective Simon Templar aka *The Saint* (no need to laugh), which is probably why I love the Volvo P1800 so much. Driven by Roger Moore in the '60s TV series, the P1800 looked superb on screen, and in fact I like them so much I bought one myself!

With gorgeous Italian styling by Frua, this cool coupé hit the road in 1961 and was even made in England in the early years. With a lack of capacity at its Swedish factory, Volvo entrusted production of the bodies to a company called Pressed Steel with final assembly taking place at Jensen, another iconic car company.

But this is an old motor and you really need to have your wits about you when you go to look at one. So, you won't be surprised when I tell you that rust can be a major problem with these (believe me I know – I had plenty to sort out on my own car!) The dreaded rot can crop-up just about everywhere so you really need to take your time when checking a potential purchase. Start at the front and check around the headlamps and grille, the inner and outer front wings and wheelarches. The bonnet can rust through at the hinges too.

You also need to look at the sills, doors, rear wings and wheelarches, and the cabin and boot floor. And while you're at it, check carefully around the front and

This is a car that looks great from any angle!

rear screens – any rust bubbling through here is a major problem. And, whatever else you do, don't forget to have a good poke around underneath as the chassis outriggers, jacking points, and front crossmember under the radiator can all get very flaky. Bear in mind, too, that as well as panels and trim parts being scarce, body repairs on the P1800 can be a tricky business so a full restoration job will cost plenty. When new, the car only came in three colours – dark grey, red, and white. So anything else means it's had a re-spray.

Better news is that engines in these motors are as tough as anything and it's not unusual for them to hit 200,000 miles before a major rebuild is necessary. Early cars came with a 1.8-litre 4-cylinder

unit with just 100bhp which later grew to 2.0-litres and 118bhp. Late models fitted with Bosch D-Jetronic injection got 130bhp which gave pretty lively performance.

There shouldn't be much to look out for either. Oil leaks aren't normally serious and, while worn valve gear can need attention above 100,000 miles, it isn't a difficult job to do. One point worth bearing in mind is that the fibre timing gears are often replaced with stronger steel ones, so it's worth asking the previous owner whether this has been done. Blue smoke from the exhaust is normally down to worn valve guides – again, not a tricky job to do. Lastly, the Bosch injection system can be a bit troublesome and replacement parts are

I reckon those chrome-topped fins look great.

Simple, stylish, and with real period charm. The P1800 cabin is a lovely place to be.

Look after it and this engine will go forever.

hard to get hold of. My advice is to go for a carburettor model.

The 4-speed manual and 3-speed automatic gearboxes were both tough and reliable and, apart from the occasional oil leak, shouldn't give any problems. If you find one with the overdrive fitted, make sure it is working properly on the test drive.

Back axles can also leak oil and, if allowed to go unrepaired, this could have caused wear in the differential which will make it noisy. You'll hear any problems on the test drive. Apart from, perhaps, a bit of play in the steering the rest of the mechanicals should be trouble free with regular maintenance. Always quiz the owner on the work that's been done.

One of the things I liked about my P1800 was the simple and stylish cabin.

You just need to check for general tattiness, signs of water leaks (look under the carpets to make sure rot hasn't set in), and things like cracked dashboard padding and door cards. Tracking down replacement trim can be time consuming and some parts are pricey so try to avoid anything too shabby. Check that all the electrical bits and pieces work as time may have taken its toll on wiring and connections.

So that's the P1800. Cool looks that stand out from the crowd and good reliability if properly looked after, it could just be the ideal sporting classic. In fact, I'm tempted to get another one!

○ Mike recommends

A cherished example in white will make you feel just like *The Saint*.

What can I say about the iconic 911. It looks fantastic and this is the perfect colour too.

Porsche 911

How could I do a book about modern classics without including the legendary 911? What an absolute icon, and so cool even Steve McQueen had one! With the famous boxer engine stuck out the back, it shouldn't have worked, but it just does. The 911 has real character and is awesome to drive. Throw in world class German engineering and you really have got the perfect classic supercar. Lots of variants over the years can make buying one a bit confusing, but it's the '930'-series Carrera introduced in 1984 that I recommend here. Targa-top and convertibles were available but, personally, I love the classic Coupé.

But you do need to be careful if you want one of these Porsches. There are absolutely loads for sale, from complete wrecks to pampered beauties and everything in between. Buy a bad one and your wallet will take a serious hammering to put it right. So research really is everything with the 911. There were lots of different models over the years, so make sure you know exactly which one you want and find out as much as possible before you go to see any cars. The UK has plenty of Porsche specialists, so get some expert advice before you start. It really will make all the difference.

As it's a Porsche, just about everything will be expensive to replace or repair so you absolutely must get one that is nice and straight. Rust protection on early cars wasn't great (later models were fully galvanised) so rot is a real concern on the 911. Repairing bodywork properly is difficult and the last thing you want is a car that has been bodged. Get an expert to take a look if you're not sure. And that

A timeless design and a Porsche badge on the nose. What could be better?

tricky handling meant quite a few got crashed by unsuspecting drivers – you want to avoid these at all costs!

There are quite a few places to check for rust, starting at the front around the headlamps, front valance and wheelarches. Left untreated, it can easily spread to the inner wings and front luggage compartment floor and then the repair bills get really serious ... There are wells either side of the engine so check

The interior design hardly changed over the years and it's built to last too. The five dial instrument pack looks superb as well. A proper Porsche.

these for rust, and fold down the back seats and look for any rot in the floor. Whatever else you do, don't rush these checks – they really are that important.

That legendary 231bhp air-cooled engine is very strong but also quite complex, so proper servicing is vital. 100,000 miles should be possible before a major rebuild, but only if previous owners haven't skimped on maintenance. Oil leaks can be common and the cooling system must be in tip-top condition to prevent overheating doing terminal damage. A good check is to grab hold of the crank pulley to check for any fore and aft movement: if it is excessive, it means too much crankshaft endfloat and a costly engine rebuild is just round the corner. On the test drive, check the oil pressure gauge to make sure everything looks healthy and watch for a flickering oil pressure warning light – anything amiss here means a big repair bill. Faulty airflow meters can cause rough-running, but these can be rebuilt at a reasonable cost. Watch out too for rotten heat exhangers – these form part of the ventilation system and you are looking at a few hundred pounds each for replacement.

Gearboxes can suffer from weak synchromesh, and later cars were fitted with the better G50 'box which was more reliable and gave a better gearchange. Make sure the 'box feels healthy on the test drive as a rebuild or replacement is a big expense. And the same goes for the clutch – a new one means taking the engine out, so any signs of slippage on the test drive should ring alarm bells.

Interiors are of excellent quality but replacement parts are costly, so avoid anything tatty and uncared for. What you want is something nice and original that the previous owner has really looked after. A bit of wear in the seats and carpets adds to character, but if too far gone you are looking at specialist re-trimmers to put it right.

The thing to remember with the 911 is that they have a huge following and that means there are lots of clubs out there that can provide support for owners. Parts and accessories are plentiful, so there really is no excuse to skimp on maintenance. Buy one of these and you will end up with one of the best classic cars ever.

◎ Mike recommends

A 1988 Carrera in Guards Red with the whale-tale spoiler and original Fuchs alloys.

Ferrari 308 GT4

If like me you dreamt as a kid of owning a supercar, then this Ferrari is definitely for you. A fantastic history and beautiful Bertone looks means the 308 has all the magic you expect from the most famous of Italian car makers. And the good news is that for something so special, prices are reasonably affordable. But they are rising all the time as people realise what a great car this is, so, if you want one, now is the time to buy!

Remember, we are talking about a Ferrari here, so any problems are going to cost big money to put right. Lots of people dreamed of owning a car like this but couldn't afford to run it properly and a bad one will be an absolute money pit.

It's a red Ferrari. Enough said!

Out of all the cars I've talked about in this book, the 308 is probably the one that needs the most care. And this is where a friendly expert will be worth their weight in gold. Whatever you do, don't jump into buying one without getting specialist advice. I really can't stress that enough. One thing you shouldn't worry about though is a car with low mileage that has had quite a few owners. This is normal with cars of this type and is rarely hiding a dodgy past.

You really need to go over the car with a fine-tooth comb, starting with the bodywork. The paintwork should be flawless as problems here will mean an expensive respray. The body panels are quite thin so can pick up dents easily, and any hint of accident damage should have you running a mile. The bonnet and boot lid on these are aluminium so rust isn't an issue on these panels, but the rest of the bodywork is steel and rot is the number one thing to look for on the GT4. Make sure you have a weak magnet handy when you inspect one of these as repairs that have been bodged using glass-fibre are a risk.

You need to be looking at the tops of the wheelarches, the sills, the bottoms of the doors, and the top of the front wings. Don't forget to have a good look at the inner front wings and the floorpan too as these are both areas where rust can really take hold. Quality body repairs will cost serious money so make sure you don't get carried away with the Ferrari magic – you need to keep your wits about you!

But the highpoint of any Ferrari is the engine, and the V8 is an absolute joy. Wow, what a noise! It's strong, too, as long as the previous owner has looked after it, but it is also complex so this is a car that really does need acres of service history to put your mind at rest. Those four twin-choke Weber carburettors can be tricky to set-up properly so watch for signs of poor running or hesitation when accelerating. Oil leaks, blue smoke from the exhaust and leaking head gaskets are things to watch out for too – remember, a full engine rebuild is going to be five figures!

The biggest job on these engines, that absolutely cannot be missed, is regular cambelt changes. Failure is an absolute disaster and a complete engine rebuild will be needed if the worst happens. Don't even think about buying one of these cars unless you see the evidence in the service history.

A corroded or leaking exhaust will cost plenty to replace, so check this carefully too. One last thing to look for is any sign of fuel leaking from either of the twin tanks – these are prone to corrosion and are not cheap to replace so don't forget to have a good look at them.

The rest of the drivetrain is pretty strong and shouldn't present any problems, though the clutch will often last only 10,000 miles or so. Once warmed up, the gearbox is a delight to snick around that lovely open gate, but difficulty selecting second gear when cold is normal. Worn brakes are costly to put right and can seize through lack of use, a weak handbrake is a common problem and rear suspension joints can wear quickly. Check the tyres for signs of uneven wear, and if the car has been standing for a while make sure the brakes feel strong on the test drive.

And it's not just the gorgeous bodywork and characterful engines that make a Ferrari so special, it's the cabins too. They really are a wonderful place to be, with plenty of soft leather and those evocative dials. The 2+2 layout even means a bit of practicality so passengers can enjoy this wonderful Italian motor as well! I think the light-coloured leather looks superb in the 308, but you do need to look out for signs of wear and tear – it will get dirty quickly and the seats can pick up scuffs on the bolsters. A thorough check will identify any problems but a caring owner should have kept the interior pristine.

Electrical issues are worth watching for too as things like lights and wipers can give problems.

I reckon the 308 really is one of the coolest cars around, and if you buy a good one ownership will be an absolute pleasure.

○ Mike recommends

A late '70s model in red with beige leather interior. The perfect combination!

Seriously quirky but the DeLorean is one of my favourite American cars, and those gullwing doors are very cool.

DeLorean DMC12

Let me take you back in time to 1985. I'm sure lots of exciting things happened that year, but what I remember most was that fantastic film *Back to the Future*. And why do I remember it so well? Because it starred one of my all-time favourite cars – the fantastic DeLorean!

Okay so the one in the film wasn't exactly standard, but I promise you will love this car because I certainly do. The

DeLorean had a difficult start and, for me, that makes it even more special. Production started in 1981 in a factory just outside Belfast, and the car was the idea of American businessman John Z DeLorean. He wanted to build a sports car that could compete with the best on the market – and he certainly came up with something special! It looked like nothing else on sale, with its gullwing doors and unpainted stainless steel bodywork, and I

85

down the country lanes in the sunshine – the MGA is a fantastic piece of British style and engineering.

But an old British classic means only one thing, and that's rust! This can be a serious problem for the MGA, so I can't tell you often enough how important it is to check a car really carefully. Even a lovely shiny example can be hiding horrors underneath so, whatever else you do, don't rush this part of the inspection. You can expect to find rot in all the usual places like the sills, floor, and doors but you should also look closely at the A-posts that support the doors as this is a notorious place for rust to set in.

To be honest, every panel is at risk with these cars, but it's the chassis where you need to pay the most attention. The first thing to do is to check the panel gaps, particularly around the doors (remember the trick I told you about with the Spitfire?) for any inconsistencies. You can expect some minor differences in panel gaps but anything major should ring alarm bells.

The next thing to do is to get underneath and check every inch of the chassis – and don't be afraid to have a good poke around under there. Small areas of rot can be repaired, but if it's gone too far the chassis could have become distorted and then you could be looking at a major restoration job. If you've got any doubts, get a specialist to take a look as it could save you an absolute fortune.

Take a good look at the paintwork and the chrome as well, as this will give you a good feel for how the car has been looked after. Does it match the seller's description and the price they are asking?

Unfortunately old cars like the lovely MGA do seem to see more than their fair share of bodged repairs and poor restorations so it pays to have your wits about you.

The B-series engine is fundamentally reliable – it came to be used in loads of different models – and is easy to repair or rebuild. Specialists can supply every part, so don't worry if the motor needs a bit of attention. The main things to check for on these engines are oil leaks, overheating caused by sludged-up cooling systems, blown head gaskets and, occasionally, a cracked cylinder head. You can get years of faithful service out of these engines if you look after them, so if you can find out that it has been pampered by the previous owner you should have few problems.

Gearboxes were a bit of a weak point though, with the synchromesh on second gear usually the first thing to go – most 'boxes will have been rebuilt by now Whining back axles and worn universal joints are also pretty common and are easily spotted on the test drive, but putting these right isn't too costly.

Watch out for leaking lever-arm dampers and bear in mind that the suspension on these cars needs regular greasing to prevent premature wear, so ask the previous owner how often this was done. A proper enthusiast owner should have kept all this stuff up to scratch, so don't be afraid to ask lots of questions. Not all cars had them, but I reckon wire wheels really suit the look of this classic British sports car; be aware though that they can give problems if they become rusty, the spokes are loose or the hub splines worn.

Specialists can rebuild wire wheels but it isn't that cheap, so factor this in to the asking price if refurbishment is needed.

I absolutely love the cabin of the MGA. It's a wonderful place to be what with all the leather and chrome, but a tired interior can really ruin the look of the car. A little bit of wear and tear all adds to the character – or 'patina' as classic car fans like to call it – but the costs will soon add up if it's too far gone. Watch out for water damage, and make sure all the electrical bits and pieces are working as they were notoriously temperamental.

If you are after something really original, bear in mind that previous owners might have been tempted to replace worn parts with bits from other models – it

pays to do your homework so you know the correct spec. And, of course, don't forget to check the hood. Good quality replacements are available at a reasonable cost, but you want to make sure the frame itself isn't damaged or corroded, as replacing these gets a bit more expensive.

So there you have the MGA. A truly fantastic British classic which I can't recommend highly enough, and a simply superb way to enjoy top-down motoring.

O Mike recommends

Finding a pampered car from an enthusiast owner who really knew how to care for this wonderful car. 'Chariot' red with wire wheels is the perfect combination.

CLASSIC 4x4s

In this chapter, I'm looking at some of my favourite vehicles – the go-anywhere 4x4s! Back in my car dealing days I bought and sold loads of these – back then 'Gullivers' in South London was one of the biggest off-roader dealers in the country – so I know what makes a good one. And, trust me, you'll absolutely love the ones I've picked. If you want a classic mud-plugger, then one of these icons is for you.

Land Rover Defender 90

What can I say about the simply legendary Land Rover Defender? With its short wheelbase, huge ground clearance, and solid engineering it really is the ultimate go-anywhere vehicle. And whether you are cruising down the King's Road or attacking a forest, the Landie can do it all. And the good news is that there are loads out there in the classifieds, so finding a good one shouldn't be difficult. But prices for old ones are on the up, so grab one while you can.

My favourite, the 90 model, hit the road in 1984 and was fitted with a 2.5-litre diesel engine pushing out a weak-sounding 68bhp. But the power didn't really matter – it's all about torque with a Landie and the 90 had plenty of that. It could tackle anything you threw at it which is why it has always been one of the best 4x4s around.

While lots of 4x4s have never been off-road, Landie owners tend to use their cars as the maker intended, so there are quite a few things to look out for before you hand over any cash. The first is rot in the chassis. Trapped mud can soon allow rust to take hold and once that's happened, a replacement chassis is normally the only answer. These aren't hugely expensive and not that hard to fit with the right tools, but as everything is nice and accessible there is no excuse not to have a good dig around underneath. While you're under there, look for damage to the chassis and drivetrain. Hard use will have left its mark, but damage should be easy to spot – the suspension can take a real hammering, too, but replacing parts is easy and cheap.

The steel bulkhead is another area where disastrous rot can take hold, so it

The iconic Land Rover in its natural habitat, but it looks good anywhere.

really does pay to check this carefully – I'd be straight back to the classifieds if things look bad here. It's more than likely that the body panels – most of which are aluminium – will have seen some abuse too, but a few dents and scrapes are all part of the character. Corrosion caused by a reaction between aluminium and steel sections is a problem, but fixable as long as it isn't too serious. Rippled panels are normal on well-used Landies so don't worry about that.

One thing I want to mention is the aftermarket scene. There are simply loads of parts available for old Land Rovers, like big wheels, extra spotlights, and bars to protect lights and bodywork, so if the car you're interested in looks a bit boring, there is plenty of scope to bring it bang up to date. Trust me, it will look awesome too!

The interior of an early Defender is what I would call basic! Seats, a steering wheel and a bit of rubber on the floor, and that's about it. But that makes it really easy for the buyer to spot any problems. Parts are cheap and easily available, so just make sure that everything works in

Chunky styling and superb in the rough stuff – what a great combination.

is built to last so there shouldn't be any major problems, and the chances are all the electrical bit and pieces should be in working order. Repairing damaged seats or carpets can get a bit pricey and you want to avoid any cars that have a damaged dash or centre console The latter gets a bit knocked about, and you're looking at around 200 pounds to refurbish a wood-trimmed one or 900 pounds for a complete replacement! If the interior is looking too battered, find another one is my advice.

The engines in the G-Wagen are as tough as old boots and capable of huge mileages if serviced properly. The 280 was fitted with Mercedes' lovely straight-six petrol engine giving a punchy 150bhp, plenty for decent performance on the road. A huge wad of bills will show the previous owner has looked after it. Watch for oil leaks from the front crankshaft pulley which is expensive to put right, but otherwise there is nothing big to worry about. You'll want to check the four-wheel drive system is healthy so have a good listen on the test drive for any horrible clunks or groans, and have a good look underneath for puddles of oil. If the gearbox or transfer box is kaput, you will be in for a four-figure bill, so don't part with any money until you are happy everything is okay.

There is only one word to describe the classy G-Wagen, and that's quality! Buy carefully and you'll get yourself a capable and solid 4x4 that should have years of life left in it.

⊙ Mike recommends

Spending just over 10k on a 1990 280GE in black or silver. Perfect!

Range Rover MkI

There is just no way I could have done this book without mentioning that off-road legend, the Range Rover. This has to be my favourite 4x4, and really is a true motoring icon. Everyone from farmers to royalty just love these cars, and you really do feel superior with that imperious driving position. The distinctive shape is part of motoring history and this is one 4x4 that is a true luxury brand.

1970 was a special year then – not only did my beloved Chelsea win the FA Cup but it was also the year that a certain Charles Spencer-King's design was revealed to the motoring public as the Range Rover – and no one had seen anything like it before. I can remember my Dad coming home one day in a mustard yellow one, and I was just so chuffed. It seemed so expensive and ostentatious back then – all the neighbours came out to have a look – but I know that every Dad would have loved to have one of these. I can't tell you how proud I felt when he drove me around in it!

But the Rangie does have its faults, and a bad one will be more trouble than it's worth, believe me. I've bought and sold loads of these over the years and spotting a bad one is pretty easy, so follow my advice and you won't go wrong.

Like all modern classics the first thing to say is buy the best you can afford. There are absolutely loads of cheap old jalopies in the classifieds, but I would definitely avoid these and so should you. While they don't rust, the alloy panels do pick up dents and scrapes but a well-cared for example should still look

Probably the greatest 4x4 of them all, and this early one still looks cool today.

smart. The main place for rot is in the steel tailgate. Even if it looks okay, open it up and give it a shake – if it rattles, it is almost certainly full of rust. Breakers yards do a roaring trade in used tailgates so replacement isn't difficult if the rest of the car is sound. The other problem affecting the tailgate is the separate rear window. The frame bows-out over time and prevents the window from latching properly, and if this happens a replacement is the only answer. Open all the doors and check the drainage holes as these get blocked and allow rot to take hold, and watch out for shiny new kick-plates on the sills. These are the perfect way to hide rust! Watch out, too, for any damage to that huge bonnet as it isn't cheap to replace.

Have a really good look underneath. Range Rovers often get used off-road, so damage to the floorpan, chassis, or suspension will be obvious, and you'll be able to spot any rot affecting the sills or floorpan. And don't worry about the big panel gaps – they were all like that!

The interior can be a bit of a disaster area on the Range Rover. Build quality was pretty awful, even when they were new, so a well-used one will be looking a bit tired. Collapsing trim and fittings are pretty normal, so you may have to look at a few before you find a nice one. Electrics were a notorious weak point so try every switch and gadget – later ones had all sorts of toys like electric seats and sunroof and bringing failed toys back to life isn't cheap. Watch out for damp and

mouldy carpets too, as weak door seals let water in. Replacement trim is pretty pricey, particularly the wood bits, and the one thing you really want to avoid is a sagging headlining. It's a common problem and an absolute nightmare to fix!

Forget the fuel bills and go for the great-sounding V8 engine, but it does need careful checking. Overheating, failed head gaskets and oil leaks from everywhere are common problems – in fact the first thing I do when I go to look at one is have a look underneath to see where the puddles of oil are! The good news, though, is that parts for these engines are plentiful and cheap so even major work won't damage the wallet too badly. I'd avoid the ridiculously thirsty 3.5-litre carburettor cars – despite a few issues with dodgy electronics, the later fuel-injected 3.9-litre engine is a much better bet.

Gearboxes are another matter though. Automatics were very popular, but make sure they change between 'Drive' and 'Reverse' smoothly – any clunks could be a failed gearbox or transfer box, and a big

repair bill is on the horizon. The same goes for manuals – any doubts on the test drive and you should start looking for another one. Automatics are heavy on brakes so check the pads and discs carefully, and check for leaks from the power steering system: another common problem.

Sagging springs and worn suspension bushes are further issues to watch out for on the test drive – if it wallows like a boat in a storm, then budget for some refurbishment.

If all this sounds like bad news, it shouldn't. While they have their faults, the Range Rover is still an outstanding classic and there is a whole world of specialists out there that can look after them properly. Updating one is easy, too, thanks to a big range of parts and accessories so you could easily end up with a real gem.

○ Mike recommends

A Vogue in that lovely Derwent blue with the 3.9-litre fuel-injected engine. You really will feel like royalty!

AMERICAN CARS

You might not know this but I absolutely love classic American cars. They look fantastic, sound superb with huge, rumbling V8 engines (the classic muscle car anyway), and I reckon are some of the coolest cars ever made.

I love a good American movie and they offer a great chance to see these cars in action – you only have to hear that wonderful exhaust note and you're transported straight to California or San Francisco! And another great thing about buying an American classic is that they have an absolutely huge following in the UK, with some great on-line communities and clubs. Go on, get involved, you'll love it!

Okay, so this is a '68 model but it still looks fantastic, and straightline performance is pretty epic too.

1970 Dodge Charger

As muscle cars go this one is an absolute legend. The awesome Dodge Charger! Like me, lots of you will remember the Charger from the brilliant *Dukes of Hazard* TV series and I couldn't resist watching it to see the 'General Lee' in action (and Daisy Duke of course!)

The Charger was everything you'd want in a muscle car. Big fastback body, big V8 engines, and that gorgeously lazy burbling exhaust note. My favourite 1970 model is from the second generation of the car and came with a variety of motors from 225 cubic inches (3.7-litres) right up to the classic 7.2-litre 440Ci. Fitted with carburettors the fuel consumption was epic, but it was worth it for all that straight-line shove and wonderful noise.

Many of the cars in the UK have been restored by now, but there are still some originals out there so it pays to be careful as they can be hiding a few disasters under shiny paintwork. Unless they have been properly treated, rust is always a risk so, whatever else you do, take your time to check every inch of that huge bodywork. Every panel needs a careful inspection, and make sure you check the floorpan, boot floor and areas like the inner wings. Good replacements won't be easy to come by, so a really rotten

That one word means serious muscle car entertainment!

You can see how pleased I am to have found one of these!

car is best avoided. Don't overlook tatty paintwork either – these really are big cars and a quality respray won't be cheap.

Try to get one that still has original trim like bumpers and light units. Speaking of lights, the headlights were hidden under electric covers (replacing a vacuum system on earlier generations) that slid up when you switched them on. It looks really cool, but these are a known weak spot and getting them working properly can take time and money.

Whenever possible, try to find a nice original example – avoid cars that have been modified or customised unless you are sure the work has been done properly.

Those big V8 engines are pretty reliable and all the parts are still available from American car specialists. Find out from the previous owner what work has

been done, but don't forget to give it the once-over anyway. Minor oil leaks should be easy to fix, but an excessively smoky exhaust or any signs of overheating are bad news so bargain hard if the motor has a few faults. Chargers were fitted with manual and auto 'boxes during their lifetime, and both are easily able to handle

I think the Charger has got more muscle ...

101

A Mustang and the open road. There is no better sight I can think of.

other work was carried out at the same time – that way you can be sure the shiny paint isn't hiding any horrors underneath. And, speaking of paintwork, owners love to customise these cars with special paint jobs and other modifications, so make sure you're happy with the end result. There are plenty of poorly modified cars and half-finished projects out there just waiting to part potential owners from their money.

Mechanically, these cars are as tough as they come. The engines and gearboxes

Behind the wheel of the brilliant Mustang. There is nowhere else I'd rather be!

can cover big mileages with proper maintenance, but like any car hard use will take its toll. So spend plenty of time talking to the previous owner and expect to see a big wad of bills for any work that's been done. The main things to watch out for are oil leaks from the engine and transmission, any sign of head gasket failure, and lots of blue smoke from the exhaust. Listen out on the test drive for whines from overworked differentials and clunks from the driveline that could indicate worn universal joints.

Don't worry too much if a bit of work needs doing as these are easy cars to work on, and there are loads of specialists out there that can supply parts. As always, it is solid bodywork that is most important.

The interior of the Mustang looks gorgeous – well I think so anyway – and there isn't much to go wrong. There aren't any gadgets like modern cars, so you are looking for things like torn seat trim, threadbare carpets and dashboard gauges that have stopped working – basically general tattiness. Find yourself a reputable specialist though and you'll be able to buy everything you need to get the cabin looking great again, so if the rest of the car is sound don't let a bit of wear and tear put you off.

◉ Mike recommends

Something nice and original with the 390Ci engine, preferably in 'Highland Green' so you too can look like Steve McQueen!

1954 Chevrolet Stepside Pickup

Nothing says America like the pickup truck. In fact, Ford's F-150 has been the

A slice of America, and what a cool motor.

Feeling pretty pleased with the lovely Stepside.

The simple chrome-rimmed dials suit the Chevy perfectly.

It might be simple, but this is one cool cabin.

biggest selling vehicle in the USA for decades which is pretty amazing. But it's not a new truck that I'm interested in – it's the classic '54 Stepside, and I just love them. This really does have to be the coolest pickup in the world and, if you want a slice of American motoring, trust me, you just have to try one of these!

Stepsides are no muscle cars – power came from a 235 cubic inch straight-six putting out a miserable sounding 112hp. It's about style though, not performance, and in this respect you won't be disappointed. Huge fenders, flashes of chrome, and whitewall tyres means the Stepside looks superb from any angle, but prices for restored pickups are really on the up, so find yourself one that needs a bit of work and bag yourself a cool American bargain!

When I say "needs a bit of work" I don't mean an absolute wreck, and there are plenty of those still for sale so you need to be careful as you could end up taking on a complete restoration. The bodywork on the '54 Stepside was pretty simple – a tough ladder chassis with welded steel cab (earlier models had the cab bolted to the chassis) – so a proper check of the condition shouldn't be difficult. Obviously you are looking for signs of rot in the chassis so have a good poke around underneath, particularly at the points where the body mounts to it and around the suspension mountings, and take a good look at all the panels. A recently imported car should be pretty sound but replacement panels are available.

Plenty of these pickups have been modified with upgraded oily bits, extra

Finished and ready to go, the Stepside looks superb.

chrome and flashy paintjobs, and, if the work has been done well, can look absolutely superb. Personally I think this sort of look really suits the superb Chevy, and there are absolutely loads of parts available from specialists if you want to create something really special.

Unless the truck you're looking at has already been restored, you can expect the mechanicals to be a bit tired. But don't worry. Engines and gearboxes (3-speed manual or auto were the choices) are generally tough and are easy to work on. You can buy all the parts you need from internet specialists, but again lots of these have been modified, so make sure you know what you're buying. The rest of the running gear was rugged and simple – drum brakes and leaf springs are the order of the day – but upgrades like disc brakes are popular with owners and can make your Chevy fit for the 21st century. Just make sure the work has been done properly.

The cabin of the Stepside is absolutely charming. Simple instruments, a bench seat and that's pretty much it. Which means it's easy to check the condition,

Looks lovely from this angle doesn't it – I just love 'em.

and even easier to make a tired interior look great again.

You've probably realised by now that I absolutely love these motors, and you'd be right. The '54 Stepside is a truly classic example of the American pickup and if this isn't one of the coolest ways to travel, I don't know what is. Try one of these and you'll fall in love with the style, so what are you waiting for!

⦿ Mike recommends

Original or modified, it doesn't matter. Just find yourself a solid example and enjoy everything this Chevy has to offer.

Simply a great motor. What more can I say?

1957 Chevrolet Bel Air

If you think the Stepside is cool, wait until you clap eyes on one of these! I almost don't know where to start with this car, but what I do know is that it's absolutely gorgeous. Huge fins, tons of chrome, burbling V8 engine – what a car!

I reckon it looks best with the 2-door bodywork, and what's more this was a very comfortable car for its time. There were absolutely loads of options for buyers to choose from – air-conditioning, power steering, power windows and seats. You name it, the Bel Air had it! Style and sophistication – what an awesome package. But the Bel Air had performance too from those big V8 engines which made it a favourite with the hot-rod and customising crowd. Buyers are prepared to pay serious prices for the best examples now so you'll need to spend some time with the classifieds to find the right car, but it will definitely be worth it.

I know I keep saying this, but rot really is the enemy of cars like these, so it pays to really take your time when inspecting a potential purchase. Better still, try to take an expert with you as it could save you a fortune in repair bills. These are big motors which can hide all sorts of nasty stuff underneath and the last thing you want is a car that's been bodged. Not only do you need to check all the panels, but get underneath and check the floor and chassis from front to back. These are real weak spots with the Bel Air and repairs here could really empty your wallet.

Take a good look too at all the exterior fittings like lights and trim, and make sure everything is present and correct.

Plenty of power under the bonnet of the lovely Bel Air.

Some parts are almost impossible to get hold of now so if you are doing any work yourself, make sure you don't break anything! Examine all the chrome as well. There is a lot of it and while some surface pitting is okay – specialists can re-chrome grilles and bumpers and all the other bits – avoid anything that is too far gone as replacement costs will soon add up. The same goes for the paintwork – a decent re-spray will cost plenty on such a big motor so bargain hard if things are looking tatty.

Engine-wise it just has to be a V8. Six-cylinder cars are cheaper but lack the performance and wonderful noise, so avoid these if possible. All the parts are available to rebuild these engines, so don't worry if a bit of work is needed though an enthusiast owner should have kept things in tip-top condition. I'd avoid the fuel-injected cars too – this was an option when the Chevy was new but wasn't very reliable and it can be expensive and time-consuming to get the car running properly. Carburettor cars are thirsty but are the better option.

The classic 3-speed column-shift manual was the standard gearbox, with a 4-speed unit as an option. An automatic 'box was a popular choice and really suits the Bel Air's easy-cruising character, so this is the one I'd go for. Two were on offer – the conventional 'Powerglide' and the 'Turboglide.' The latter was complex and not that reliable so is best avoided.

Drum brakes and vague steering are all part of the charm, and as long as they haven't been neglected shouldn't give any problems. Like many American classics

A wonderful picture and a wonderful car.

Just makes you want to jump in and cruise ...

An absolutely beautiful interior – the fluffy dice are optional!

upgrades are popular so make sure you know what's been fitted.

And the interior? Absolutely wonderful and full of '50s American charm. As I've already mentioned, there were loads of extras available when this car was new so it pays to check everything carefully. Make sure everything works as bringing some of the gadgets back to life could get seriously expensive. There are plenty of specialists out there that can help with re-trimming a tired interior, so don't worry if seats and carpets are looking past their best, and it might be an opportunity to personalise things a bit if you fancy a bit of customising.

I love everything the Bel Air has to offer and this might just be one of the coolest cars out there.

Just look at those fins! Gorgeous.

◉ Mike recommends

Avoiding restoration cases, finding yourself a tidy automatic V8, and hitting the open road!

Pure American chrome takes you straight back to the '50s.

Willys Jeep

Simple, rugged, and iconic. I can only be talking about the legendary Willys Jeep. If you love a good war film – and I certainly do – then you'll be familiar with this fantastic classic. Based on a design by the American Bantam Car Company, more than 600,000 of these awesome off-roaders were built (most were made by Willys Overland Motors but quite a few were also made by Ford). Designed to be light and tough, the Jeep was the ultimate go-anywhere vehicle and a huge number still survive today thanks to an army of dedicated military enthusiasts.

Prices start at about 4k for a useable example, but the best and rarest cars can fetch up to 15k, so there is bound to be one to fit your budget.

There is an absolute wealth of expertise out there for these vehicles so there really is no excuse for landing yourself with a duff one. Do your homework, find a knowledgeable specialist and grab yourself a true motoring icon.

So what do you need to watch out for? Well despite being as tough as they come, the body and chassis can suffer over time so don't rush into anything. The first thing to look for is any damage to the chassis – over-enthusiastic off-roading can leave them bent out of shape which is pretty disastrous, so find another one if it's looking battered.

The Willys Jeep is an absolute legend and I just love it.

Rot can set in, and the wings, fuel tank, and floor panels are particularly at risk, so have a good poke around underneath. The good news is that the Jeep couldn't be easier to rebuild with new panels, and even complete new bodies, still available so minor panel damage isn't a deal-breaker. In fact, they made enough spares to build every car 15 times over so you shouldn't have any trouble finding the part you need!

Plenty come with all the military extras too like spare fuel cans and shovels, so you shouldn't have any trouble finding something original.

The Jeep was designed to be easy to repair in tough conditions, so the mechanicals are simple and robust which

is great news for the used buyer. Engines were simple side-valve units that made 60hp from their 2.2-litres. Stuck on the back was a 3-speed gearbox and 2-speed transfer box, and while they might be unrefined, they are incredibly tough. Engine blocks can crack, but one of the main problems is oil leaks from both the engine and transmission but these are rarely serious and you can expect a bit of exhaust smoke as well. Don't worry though as worn out units are cheap and easy to rebuild.

The parts supply for these Jeeps is simply brilliant – just about everything you could need is available – so a car that is fundamentally sound can easily be bought up to scratch. Drum brakes and

Ready to jump aboard and pretend I'm in my favourite war film.

leaf springs are low tech but perfect for the job and shouldn't give any bother with regular maintenance. The steering is heavy at low speeds, and if it seems particularly bad could be a sign that the steering box or joints are seizing up. Lubrication could cure this, but replacement is a cheap and easy option.

The last thing to mention here is the electrics – most original Jeeps had a 6-volt system but many owners have upgraded this to the modern 12-volt system. It's a useful update so worth checking if it's been done on the example you're looking at.

I'd like to tell you all about the interior, but there isn't much of an interior to talk about! A few instruments, some seat padding, and a simple fabric hood and that's your lot. You'll soon see what sort of condition it's in and getting hold of replacement bits is easy. So concentrate on finding a solid, rust-free example and enjoy one of the most iconic vehicles ever made. Going off-road has never been so much fun!

○ Mike recommends

Finding an enthusiast-owned example with all the military extras and you don't need to ask about the colour ...

MIKE'S FAVOURITE CLASSICS

There are just so many wonderful modern classics out there, I couldn't possibly have fitted them all in. I absolutely recommend the cars I've already told you about – you won't be disappointed with any of them – but this chapter is just about my other personal favourites.

No particular order, just the cars I really love. And if you wanted to buy one of these instead, well I wouldn't blame you.

VW Beetle

What's not to like about such an iconic car? Tough, simple, and with bags of character, the Beetle is one of the all-time greats. Unbelievable to think it all started back in 1945 with Beetles still rolling off Mexican production lines well into the 21st century. Early cars are rare and really sought after now, so I'd be looking for a nice original car from the mid '70s. A car like this will still have all the Beetle charm and you'll be able to pick up a well looked after car without breaking the bank. One of my favourite models is the 'Jeans' special edition, which came with special body decals and seat trim that looked like denim. A really cool car, but not that many were made so definitely worth looking out for in the classifieds.

Volkswagen sold millions of these things so there is an absolutely huge number out there on the used market, everything from restoration basket-cases to pampered enthusiast-owned motors. Prices vary a lot so it really pays to do your homework on the fantastic 'Bug.' There are some real bargains out there, but many will be wrecks and only fit for the breakers yard! My advice is to go and see plenty before you part with any cash – that way, you'll know exactly what to look for. Trust me, the perfect Beetle is out there somewhere just waiting for you to snap it up!

But the fabulous Beetle is an old car, so there is still plenty to watch out for and rust is perhaps the biggest enemy. Just about every panel can suffer from rot, particularly the running boards, sills and floorpan as well as around suspension mountings. When you've found the car you want, really

Simple, rugged, and with bags of character. That'll be the iconic Beetle.

quiz the owner on any bodywork repairs that might have been done – most have had new panels at some point in their lives and you want to make sure the repairs are top-notch. The good news is that decent quality pattern replacements are cheap and fairly easy to fit, but it pays to take an expert along to make sure there are no horrors lurking underneath.

One of the things I love about these cars is the charming and simple cabin. There is just about nothing to go wrong in there, other than tatty seats and carpets. Even then, replacements are easy and cheap to source from the internet so a tired interior can easily be transformed into as-new condition.

The air-cooled engine slung out-back is almost unburstable and perfect for tuning. Parts are cheap and the engines are easy to work on, so, as long as they have been serviced regularly, should give years of reliable service. You'll need to check for any oil leaks, and make sure there isn't an excessive amount of blue smoke from the exhaust which can mean worn cylinder bores. Rebuilding one of these characterful engines isn't hard though, and is definitely something you can tackle yourself with a decent set of tools. Lastly, make sure there are no signs of overheating – these engines use a system of flaps to control the flow of cooling air, and the mechanism is prone to seizing-up over time. It isn't hard to fix but faulty operation might have damaged the engine if the previous owner ignored the problem.

Gearboxes are tough and only worn synchromesh can be an issue at high mileages – don't worry, though, as reconditioned 'boxes aren't too costly.

Worn suspension and steering is common on neglected cars but, again, parts are cheap and it's an easy job to bring it up to scratch. A good test drive will show up any nasty problems in this area, but remember to bargain hard if you think the car needs work.

Maybe the best thing of all is that there is a whole industry dedicated to the 'Bug' and every part and accessory you can imagine is available. Whether you want something completely original or a bit more special, the choice is yours. There is a great owner's club scene too and you can really enjoy owning VW's legend.

The Beetle might be slow, but with such charm and character, who cares! Find yourself a well-cared for car and I guarantee you won't be disappointed.

Citroën DS

No doubt in my mind, this is one of the most beautiful cars ever built. The DS was launched at a time when all other cars were thoroughly conventional, and to the thousands who saw it at motor shows it must have seemed like it had come from outer space! It looks like nothing else even

Possibly the coolest looking classic on the planet, and full of clever technology too.

With a cabin as quirky as the bodywork, this is Gallic style at its very best.

today, and is the most stylish way to travel I can imagine. Even my teenage daughter loves these, they really are that cool!

The gorgeous DS (pronounced as 'déesse' in French, meaning 'goddess') first amazed us way back in 1955 and continued in production for twenty years – it was even made here in Blighty for a while in that well known car manufacturing hotspot, Slough! Citroën sold nearly 1.5 million of these futuristic cars, and they were absolutely stuffed full of clever innovations that are still impressive today. On some models there were swivelling headlights so you could see round corners, fully powered hydraulic suspension, steering and brakes, and even a clutchless semi-automatic gearbox. The DS really was ahead of its time.

The good news is that prices for good ones are rising all the time, so buy carefully and your car will only appreciate in value. There is a great owner's club and plenty of specialists, so expert advice is

never far away. In fact, I'd be tempted to buy a left-hooker from France, ideally a long-wheelbase model in full-on 'Pallas' specification. Don't worry about the left-hand drive either, it just adds even more charm to this already characterful car.

The DS is a complex car, so, if you're not confident, it really does pay to find an expert. Rust and rot could easily leave you with a restoration case – the boot floor and rear inner wings, door bottoms, windscreen and headlamp surrounds, and fuel tank area are all at risk of rotting away. A rotten car will cost an absolute fortune to put right, so it really does pay to find a solid example. Find out as much as you possibly can about the DS, and when you find one take someone with you who knows them – they could save you a lot of money.

The complicated suspension and hydraulics aren't for the faint-hearted,

My Edd says these are tricky to work on so you might need a bit of patience!

so this is one area that you want to be in tip-top condition before parting with any cash. Good news is that the engines are tough, so, as long as it's been looked after, shouldn't cause any major headaches. What probably will give you a massive headache though is doing any repairs! I've got to tell you, the DS isn't the easiest car to work on, so you'll need plenty of patience, but it will be worth it just to have one of these wonderful Gallic motors in your garage. Oh, and listen for whining gearboxes and watch out for dodgy semi-automatics if you want to avoid big bills.

If anything does go wrong, you won't need to panic as there are lots of knowledgeable specialists out there and replacement parts won't break the bank.

Another thing I love about these cars is the interior. It's just as stylish and unusual as that swoopy body, and is a really wonderful place to be. A well-cared for car should be in decent condition with no major damage to trim and fittings, but bringing a tatty example up to scratch isn't difficult. Just about every part is available from specialists, so if the rest of the car is solid, don't let a tatty cabin put you off. A few minutes on the internet and you'll be able to find everything you need to bring back the smart looks that the wonderful DS deserves.

Don't let this talk of complexity put you off. My advice is to get as late a car as possible – a DS21 with the fuel-injected engine would be perfect. Find a good one, get friendly with a local specialist and you really will end up owning one of the coolest cars ever designed.

Ford Capri MkIII

"The car you always promised yourself" the advertisement said, and when the Capri was launched it was light years away from the unadventurous Cortina. Thousands of motorists bought into the dream of owning the classy coupé, and it remains one of Ford's most successful cars. And it's not hard to see why. I just love the style of the Capri, and with so many around on the used market you can bag yourself a lovely example for very little money. My favourite is definitely the stylish MkIII which hit the road back in 1978. As a teenager, I couldn't wait for Saturday night when I could watch *The Professionals* screeching around London in the cool Ford – I'm sure that's why I love them so much!

The Capri is just so straightforward, bad ones are easy to spot with just a few basic checks. Like many British cars of the period, rust was the main enemy and appeared in all the usual places – the sills and wheelarches were particularly prone, along with the top of the front suspension turrets. There won't be many around that haven't been repaired here at one time or another. There are plenty of bodged and abused ones around at bargain money, but avoid these unless you really want a restoration project. With so many to choose from in the classifieds, it's easy to find one that has been cared for by an enthusiast owner.

It is unbelievable to think that Ford even stuck a tiny 1.3-litre engine under that gorgeous long bonnet – you could almost get in there with it as there was so much spare room! Things got better with the tough 2.0-litre 'Pinto' engine, and

A bit more stylish than a Cortina wouldn't you say?

better still with the brawny 3.0-litre V6. But for me, the best model was always the later 2.8-litre injected V6. Known as the 'Cologne' engine, 160bhp was enough to shove the Capri to 60mph in around 8.5 seconds, and it sounded absolutely fantastic – everything a stylish coupé should be.

The interior is basic by modern standards – manual mirrors and sunroof and a radio/cassette were about it – but ideal if you're looking for a simple classic. You don't have to worry about stuff like electric windows and central locking as Ford never fitted these, though quite a few cars were fitted with aftermarket kits (make

Looks superb from this angle, and I reckon those later alloys really suit it.

Lovely simple cabin but the half-leather Recaro seats really lift the ambience.

sure these work properly, though, as fixing them can be a bit of a nightmare). Those velour-covered Recaro seats are lovely (later cars even came with part-leather trim), and it really is just a case of making sure everything works. Parts are cheap and it's easy to upgrade the interior to the later spec if you fancy it, so you could even buy a car with a tatty interior, so long as it's reflected in the price.

Engines are nice and simple to work on, every mechanic can repair them, and they are perfect for the DIY-er. What could be better? That favourite V6 is a tough engine too – the only things to watch out for are oil leaks, signs of blown head gaskets and rough-running caused by tired injection systems. A smoky exhaust on start-up normally just means worn

valve-stem oil seals, a common fault and not hard to fix. Just avoid any thrashed or modified cars – nice and original is best. The earliest cars came with a 4-speed gearbox, but try to get a later car with the 5-speed unit as it makes the car much more useable. The differential can get a bit rumbly – easy to spot on a test drive – but a reconditioned unit isn't expensive so don't worry too much.

Power steering systems can get a bit leaky, and worn suspension bushes and sagging leaf springs are common on neglected cars. These parts are cheap, though, so refreshing a tired example isn't costly.

The Capri is a true British icon, so find yourself a nice original 2.8i and you'll see why I love them so much.

Quite possibly the perfect British sports car, a well-sorted Elan is a real delight on a quiet country road.

Lotus Elan

Almost certainly the inspiration for the awesome MX-5, the Elan had everything you could want in a sports car. Light weight, agile handling and a revvy little twin-cam engine: nothing made you feel more connected to the road. Get one of these on an empty country road and you will absolutely fall in love with it. I've driven a few of these in my time, and the performance and handling are a brilliant reminder of what driving a great British classic is all about. When I was growing up in London, it was always a real treat to see one of those cracking little sports cars on the road, and I've wanted one ever since!

Introduced in 1962, the Elan really was all about Lotus-founder Colin Chapman's philosophy of "adding lightness," weighing-in at just 700kg. With 105bhp

from the 1.6-litre twin-cam, performance was superb and the later 'Sprint' with 126bhp was a true road-rocket!

Despite superb Lotus engineering, these are old-school classics and there is plenty to watch out for if you want to bag a good one. That glass-fibre bodywork is easily damaged, with cracks and crazing common. Any faults should be easy to see, but remember repairs are a specialist business and previous owners may have been tempted to bodge them to save money – get an expert opinion if you're not sure.

The separate chassis is prone to rot too, and while galvanised replacements aren't that expensive, it's a fiddly job to do. You really do need to get right underneath and poke around to make sure everything is solid – not easy with

automatic gearbox. Many people didn't like these but that engine sounds amazing and made the gorgeous Jag lovely and easy to drive.

The rest of the running gear needs just as careful an inspection. There are loads of joints in the suspension and steering that can wear out or seize-up and replacement will take a lot of labour time. And while wire wheels give a classic period look worn hubs and splines are a common problem – these can be repaired by specialists, but it's not a cheap job. I say it a lot in this book but if you're not sure always get an expert to check a car over.

Just about every part is available, but prices are high so there really is no way to repair an E-type cheaply. That's why finding a good one is so important. But spend the right sort of money, and you'll have bagged yourself one of the world's greatest sports cars. There really is nothing like the E-type Jaguar.

Morgan Plus 8

They might look old-fashioned, but I just love the classic Morgan. A true British sports car in every way, the Morgan is still hand-built and has hardly changed over the years. Squeeze yourself into that lovely cockpit and get the top down and you'll feel like a World War 1 fighter pilot! Perhaps that's why I like them so much?

The 4-4, the company's first four-wheeler, was launched way back in 1936

Underneath those old-fashioned looks is a true sports car. This is hand-crafted Britishness at its very best.

with a steel chassis and body panels and an ash wood frame; a tradition they stayed with for many years. It wasn't until 1954 that the shape we know today hit the road with that lovely curved radiator grille sitting up front. Long waiting lists for new cars mean used ones still fetch high prices, so you will need to search long and hard for a bargain. Morgan's are usually owned and driven by enthusiasts so tend to be well cared for, which is great news for the second-hand buyer.

Even older cars should still be in excellent condition, but doesn't mean there aren't a few things to watch out for. The separate chassis and ash wood frame (treated with a better preservative from the mid-'80s) are generally long-lasting, but rot can set in. Repairs to the wood frame are for specialists only, but a new chassis can be bought for less than a thousand pounds. Bear in mind though that fitting it is a huge task, even for the experienced mechanic, so get an expert to take a look before committing yourself.

Those lovely curving wings can pick up stone chips and such a wonderful car deserves a top-notch respray, so you'll need to factor in the cost if the paintwork is looking tired.

The traditional interiors are very individual, and no two are likely to be exactly the same. They are simple to look after, though, and as long as water damage hasn't ruined the wood or leather, shouldn't be a problem. Don't forget to check the hood though. Even though it was a quality item when new, time can take its toll and a proper Morgan replacement is seriously costly. Another thing to remember is that plenty of buyers chose to personalise their car too, with special paint and trim colours and extras like chrome luggage racks for that authentic period charm. You might need to look at a few examples before you find the one that suits you.

Morgan have used a variety of engines over the years from a humble Ford unit to the thumping Rover V8 that wowed the crowds at the 1968 Earls Court Motor Show. Even Fiat engines have found their way under that beautifully crafted bonnet. All are fairly simple to work on with good parts availability, and if the car has been serviced properly shouldn't be anything to worry about. Without a doubt, my favourite is the V8 – it can get the lightweight Morgan down the road at a fair old pace, with a lovely noise to go with it. It's a reliable lump too – just watch out for any signs of oil leaks, or overheating that could have done for the head gaskets.

The rest of the driveline is similarly straightforward but the suspension remained quite old-fashioned – it used a 'sliding pillar' arrangement with a variety of joints and bushes that required regular greasing. A careful previous owner should have seen to this as a matter of course.

Wire wheels were another popular choice and, while they look fantastic, can cause a few headaches if they aren't looked after. There are plenty of specialists out there that can rebuild them – it's definitely a job for the experts – but factor in the cost if they are looking a bit unloved.

Simple and traditional, the Morgan makes a superb sports car and one you really should try. You'll love it.

INDEX